ZEUS
GRANTS
STUPID
WISHES

ZEUS GRANTS STUPID WISHES

◆ ◆ ◆

A No-Bullshit Guide to World Mythology

CORY O'BRIEN

ILLUSTRATIONS BY SARAH E. MELVILLE

A PERIGEE BOOK

A PERIGEE BOOK
Published by the Penguin Group
Penguin Group (USA) Inc.
375 Hudson Street, New York, New York 10014, USA

USA / Canada / UK / Ireland / Australia / New Zealand / India / South Africa / China

Penguin Books Ltd., Registered Offices: 80 Strand, London WC2R 0RL, England
For more information about the Penguin Group, visit penguin.com.

Library of Congress Cataloging-in-Publication Data

O'Brien, Cory.
Zeus grants stupid wishes : a no-bullshit guide to world mythology / Cory O'Brien ;
illustrations by Sarah E. Melville.— First edition.
pages   cm
ISBN 978-0-399-16040-0
1. Mythology—Humor.   I. Melville, Sarah E., illustrator.   II. Title.
BL311.O25 2013
201'.30207—dc23   2012042666

First edition: March 2013

PRINTED IN THE UNITED STATES OF AMERICA

10 9 8 7 6 5 4 3 2 1

While the author has made every effort to provide accurate telephone numbers, Internet
addresses, and other contact information at the time of publication, neither the
publisher nor the author assumes any responsibility for errors, or for changes that occur
after publication. Further, the publisher does not have any control over and does not
assume any responsibility for author or third-party websites or their content.

Most Perigee books are available at special quantity discounts for bulk purchases for
sales promotions, premiums, fund-raising, or educational use. Special books, or book
excerpts, can also be created to fit specific needs. For details, write: Special Markets,
Penguin Group (USA) Inc., 375 Hudson Street, New York, New York 10014.

To Tiresias Chang
*For giving me the idea for this whole
thing in the first place.*

And to Christina Sheldon
*I met you in a bar when I was thirteen
and promised to dedicate my first book to you.
You probably thought I was joking.*

CONTENTS

EGYPTIAN

MAYAN

JUDEO-CHRISTIAN

HINDU

JAPANESE

INTRODUCTION

*(Or, the Part of This Book You Can
Safely Tear Out If You Need to Make It
Slightly Lighter for Some Reason)*

'Sup, guys.

Here is a book I wrote, and I hope you enjoy it. A lot of what is in it comes from my website, which is on the Internet, but there is a lot of stuff that is only in this book too, like this introduction. So I figure I better use this opportunity to say some things about myths, and the writing thereof.

First off, I think anybody who complains that a retelling of a myth is "inaccurate" doesn't really understand what it means to retell a myth, or probably even what a myth *is*. (Yes, there are some non-canon additions in this book. I'm sure you'll spot a few.) I always stay true to the general arc of the story, but my retellings aren't always canon in the obsessive fanboy sense.

I have spent the last three years frantically accumulating mythological knowledge and distilling it into what some have affectionately called "the death of intellectualism." I am proud of this, because I think that lately, myths have suffered from a severe intellectualism overdose. Everybody's always studying them in school, or reading watered-down versions of them to little kids, and what that means is that hardly anybody has the time to actually sit down and look at how fucking *funny* these things are. I mean, for a long, LONG time, the difference between a good story and a bad story was whether a bard could memorize it well enough to not get eviscerated by a mead hall full of drunken barbarians. These things are holy, sure, in a way. But they are *definitely* designed to cater to the lowest common denominator.

Speaking of common denominators, one of the guys who I read a lot of while I was making this book was a dude named Joseph Campbell. He wrote a book called *The Hero with a Thousand Faces*, which is both an incredibly sweet title and an incredibly insightful book. One of the things he spends a lot of time talking about is how similar the mythologies of different cultures are, and how that arises out of our innate neurological similarities as human beings (you'll see what I mean when you get a ways into this book).

What I think is particularly interesting, though, and what I wanted to talk about here, is one of the things he says in *his* introduction, which is that a lot of the psychological problems that we experience today may stem from our rejection of mythology. Like, if this stuff came out of our common human brain problems, isn't it kind of dangerous to pretend that they're no longer relevant? I mean, sure, they're a little outdated, but that's where *I* come in, my friends.

We can rebuild these myths. We have the technology. We can make them snappier, flashier ... it would be hard to make them sexier ... But you get where I'm going with this. It's been too long since someone snatched these myths out of the past and pitched them screaming into our everyday lives.

In *The Hero with a Thousand Faces*, Joseph Campbell

says that the role of the ancient priest, the role of guiding people through their spiritual crises with mythology, has been taken over by the modern psychologist. Well, I'm no psychologist, but I once talked to one for almost ten minutes at a grocery store, so come on: Let me massage your brain with my myths.

GREEK

Ahhh, the Greeks
dead longer than America has even existed
and still invading our lives with their myths.
If you drive a car
you may have bought auto parts from Midas.
If you listen to Internet radio
you might be acquainted with Pandora.
If you got laid today
you might have spotted a Trojan on the condom
if you use condoms
which you should
but if you don't
then you're probably a lot like Zeus and/or Aphrodite
SO YOU CAN'T ESCAPE THESE MYTHS NO
    MATTER WHAT.
My friends, the extent to which we idolize these Greek
    myths is ridiculous.
Poets can't stop talking about them
we carve crazy Greek-looking columns into all our
    national monuments
we name our planets after (the Roman versions
    of) them
and NOW
you are about to get the inside scoop on them.

◆ ◆ ◆

CRONUS LIKES TO
EAT BABIES

So everybody knows Zeus is the king of the gods
right?

WRONG.

I mean, he is the king of the gods
but first of all, not everybody knows that
and second of all
he wasn't *always* the king of the gods.
Because, see, for a while there was this guy Uranus
who was a total asshole
(haha, Uranus)
anyway he was the king of the gods, born out of the sky
or maybe it was the aether?
but either way he was definitely married to Gaia
who some sources say *also* gave birth to him
so . . . awkward.

BUT LIKE I WAS SAYING
Uranus bones Gaia a bunch
because it is basically just him and Gaia
alone in the universe
and what else are they gonna do?
And they have a whole bunch of kids
but then Uranus suddenly decides he hates all of
     the kids
and instead of like

giving them up for adoption or something
he just decides to try and STUFF THEM ALL BACK
    INTO HIS WIFE
like "THESE ARE NOT THE BABIES I ORDERED
I AM RETURNING THEM TO THE
    BABYSTORE."
Which I think demonstrates a really shocking lack of
    understanding
of how babies are made.

Now, Gaia is the entire Earth, you understand
so this would be fine if they were like
normal-sized children
you know, like BABIES or something
but they are not babies
they are TITANS.
OW.

So all these titans are writhing around in Gaia's womb
going nuts
and Gaia gets seriously fed up with this nonsense
and tells one of them
whose name is Cronus
"Hey, Cronus
why don't you and your candy-assed brothers
get out of my womb
and do something useful, like murder your father?"
and Cronus says "How 'bout I do you one better
and saw off his balls?"
and Gaia says "That sounds like a fantastic plan!
Here, have my ball-sawing scythe!"

So one night Uranus is about to get busy with Gaia
again
I guess so he can father another baby
and then stuff it back into her

but instead of getting sex
he gets a SURPRISE PENISECTOMY
Cronus all jumping out from behind a rock
like "HAHA, GOT YOUR DICK, DAD."
Which is something no son should ever have to say to
his father.
Then Uranus's dick falls into the ocean
and makes a whole ton of foam
and that is where Aphrodite comes from eventually
from dick foam.
You know that painting with her standing on the shell
with all the angels and stuff?
Dick foam.
All of it.

So then Cronus is king of the gods suddenly
the gods being actually the other titans
including some dudes called the Cyclopes
who you probably know about already
(they are the ones with the congentially poor depth
perception)
and also some other dudes called the Hecatoncheires
who are significantly less talked about
because they have A HUNDRED HANDS EACH
AND THAT IS TERRIFYING.
So naturally Uranus especially hated these freaks
when he was king.
And part of Cronus's whole campaign platform for
killing Uranus
was that he was totally gonna free those dudes
but no sooner is he king than he goes PSYCH
and stuffs them right back into Gaia's cooch AGAIN.
So obviously Gaia is pretty sore about this whole thing
and then to make matters worse
an oracle tells Cronus that his kid is gonna kill him.
and he's like "OH SHIT

WHICH KID?
I'VE GOT LIKE A GAZILLION KIDS
I NEED TO CUT DOWN
MAYBE I SHOULD STUFF THEM INTO MY—
waaaait a second
I'm becoming my father."

So instead Cronus comes up with a more sensible
    alternative
which is to stuff all his kids into his STOMACH
but the fact that he is eating his kids
does nothing to stop him from banging his wife
Rhea
because when you are king of the gods
banging is what you do.
So she keeps having kids
and he keeps demanding to eat them
but after a while she catches on to his crafty prank
and when she gives birth to Poseidon
she's like "That's weird, I gave birth to a horse instead
    of a kid. Whoops."
And Cronus has no reason to disbelieve her because hey
if Aphrodite can come from dick foam
why can't Rhea pop out a horse?
So he eats the horse instead of Poseidon
and then he gets Rhea preggers AGAIN
and this time she is pregnant with ZEUS
and when Cronus is like "HEY, WIFE
SERVE ME UP A DOUBLE-CHILDREN
    CHEESEBURGER
WITH WAFFLE FRIES AND EXTRA PLACENTA"
she is super crafty and just takes a big rock
dresses it up like a baby
and then feeds it to Cronus
all like "Man, my womb is sure serving up some crazy
    stuff lately, huh?"

But Cronus catches on to that prank pretty fast
and starts running around
putting random parts of the world in his mouth
hoping to find the one that has his son in it
so Rhea is like "Hey, Zeus
you know what you should do?
You should go free those freaky mutant titans your dad
    imprisoned
and use them to murder your dad."
And Zeus says, "I'll do you one better:
how 'bout instead of killing him
I make him vomit up all my siblings
and then I just kinda . . .
imprison him somewhere?"
and Rhea is like "Well, it isn't very brutal
but it *is* kinda gross. So okay."
So Zeus and those ugly one-eyed dudes and the *really*
    ugly hundred-handed dudes
all siege the crap out of Cronus
and then they stick their fingers down his throat
and he barfs up all the gods and goddesses
or at least a lot of them
(the rest of them get born later)
and then Zeus is the king of the gods
and those titan dudes are still ugly
so Zeus ends up imprisoning them all again.

So the moral of the story
is that if you are not ready to be a father
consider all of your options
before skipping directly to cannibalism.

◆ ◆ ◆

Zeus Sticks It to Semele a Little Too Hard

So Zeus is just cruisin' around, right
pickin' mortal women to bone
and he sees this priestess named Semele in one of his
    temples
sacrificing this bull
and then swimming naked in a river
(to wash off all that blood)
HOT.
So Zeus
who is an eagle right now
and also a super creepy voyeur
is like WHOA BABY
GOTTA GET ME SOME OF THAT
and immediately starts having an affair with her.

Now Hera finds out about this
like she always does.
I mean, first of all
after the number of women Zeus has slept with
this chick has got to have like
spidey senses for infidelity
not that Zeus makes ANY EFFORT AT ALL to cover
    his tracks
and second of all, why is Hera still his wife?
I mean is he just *so incredibly unfaithful*
that it wraps around
and he is actually a good husband?

Anyway, Hera finds out about this latest sexcapade
and instead of divorcing her husband
she decides to prank him.

So she goes down to Earth and finds Semele
and she's like "Hey, I'm Zeus's wife."
and Semele is like "AAAAH DON'T KILL ME"
and Hera is like "Hahaha I'm not going to kill you.
I am fine with my husband's infidelity for some
    reason.
In fact I just wanted to let you know
that he and I have WAYYYY better sex than you
    and him."
And Semele says "I dunno, man
we have had some pretty epic boner adventures."
And Hera says "Oh honey, you don't even *know*.
Next time you two are doing the horizontal
    monster mash
ask him to stick it to you like he sticks it to ME."
So Semele says "Hmm, okay
you can't possibly have any ulterior motives for telling
    me this.
I'll do it."

So next time she and Zeus get busy
she is like "Hold on there, bad boy
make love to me like you make love to your WIFE."
and Zeus is like "Aww man, way to kill the mood.
Look, if I did that, you would explode."
and Semele, thinking that he is speaking figuratively
is like "Come on, handsome, I can take it.
and anyway, I totally won't believe you're Zeus unless
    you do this."
and Zeus is like "WHAT? NO, I'M TOTALLY ZEUS
WHO SAYS I'M NOT?"
and he turns into lightning

and sets her on fire
and she explodes
and Zeus is like "Aww dammit
I knew this was gonna happen.
Now I gotta save the baby I was keeping inside of her
especially since I'm pretty sure my wife is gonna try
    and eat it or something."
so Zeus grabs the baby
as it flies out of its mother's exploding corpse
and he thinks real fast and sews it up in his thigh
and then after a few months
of walking VERY awkwardly
and avoiding his wife even more than he already does
he goes and hides in a cave
and gives birth to this baby out his thigh
and this baby is none other
than Dionysus
the god of drinking so hard you wake up with TWO
    hangovers and then they FIGHT.
And later
when Dionysus grows up
he goes and frees Semele from Hades
and makes her a goddess
with a different name for some reason
(Thyone)
maybe so Hera won't go catfight her ass.

So basically what this story teaches us
is that when you are having sex
you should never be lightning

but that's not the last tomfoolery Dionysus finds
    himself in the middle of.
Oh no, my friends.
Read on . . .

❖ ❖ ❖

King Midas Is:
GOLDFINGER

So one day, Dionysus wakes up from a drunken stupor
to find his foster father missing.
This surprises no one
because, see, Dionysus would not stand
for having a foster father
who was not some kind of alcoholic satyr
and so naturally the two of them just get shitfaced
like all the time
and Dionysus doesn't even need to worry about being
    hung over at school
'cause his alcoholic foster father
IS ALSO HIS SCHOOLMASTER.
His name is Silenus, by the way. He's awesome.
Anyway, Dionysus wakes up one day
and Silenus is not there
because he got real hammered and passed out in a rose
    garden
which happened to belong to this king named Midas.

Now, Midas is a pretty good king
and I will tell you why:
It is because when he finds some drunk satyr
passed out in his rose garden
he does not get all butthurt about it and call the
    guards.
No, he invites the guy inside
and makes him some sandwiches

and lets him crash on his couch for TEN DAYS
while he nurses his epic hangover
at which point he gives him a ride home to Dionysus's
        place
and Dionysus is all "NICE
YOU BROUGHT MY DAD BACK.
Do you want a beer?"
And Midas is all "No thanks, man, I gotta drive home."
And Dionysus is like "Well, I want to do *something* to
        thank you
but all I've got are these beers and these wishes."
And Midas is like "I WISH FOR EVERYTHING I
        TOUCH TO TURN TO GOLD."
and Dionysus is like "DONE."
And then he and his dad go off to get trashed again
and probably get lost
and end up granting some more ridiculous wishes
because that is how they do.

Anyway, Midas gets home and is like "GENTLEMEN
PREPARE ME A MARVELOUS FEAST."
And he sits down at his ludicrous feast table
and he picks up this big ol' leg of mutton
but before he can put it in his mouth
IT TURNS INTO GOLD
and he is like "OH NO.
Well, at least I can still get drunk."
And he picks up his wineglass
which turns to gold, obviously
and he downs his wine
except that when it goes into his mouth
it also turns into gold
and probably chokes him.
Maybe he even throws up in his mouth a little
but if he does
that shit TURNS TO GOLD.

AWESOME.
Actually I'm not sure what's keeping all of Midas's
    organs and bodily fluids
from turning his body into a California Gold Rush of
    suffering
but thank gods for the little things, right?

Anyway, King Midas is pretty hungry and thirsty
and he can't think of anything to do about this shit
so he goes into his house
and just starts turning everything into gold
because gods dammit
if he's gonna starve to death
at least he is gonna starve to death in a weird gold
    house
and he gets so caught up in doing this
that he does not notice his daughter come into
    the room
and his daughter loves him so much
that she just wants to surprise him with a BIIIG HUG
only she is the one who gets surprised
'CAUSE HER ASS GETS TURNED TO GOLD
not just her ass either
her whole body, and also her clothes.
Also, she is not the only one who is surprised
Midas is pretty surprised too
because he has just accidentally killed his daughter
but also made her like a billion times more valuable.
Seriously, who needs kids
when you have solid gold statues of your kids?
But Midas doesn't see it that way
because he has some kind of weird parent thing.

So he starts crying
and his tears probably turn into gold
which is incredibly uncomfortable

and just makes him cry more
but finally he gets ahold of himself and he's like "HEY DIONYSUS
COME FIX THIS SHIT FOR ME."
and Dionysus is like "What? Oh shit.
What have you done, man.
What is it with you mortals always starving to death
and petrifying your daughters?"
Okay, well, I guess what you can do
is go bathe in this river called Pactolus
and that will solve your problems."
so Midas does that, and it takes away his superpower
while simultaneously turning all the sand in the
     river gold
but does nothing to fix the fact
that Midas's daughter is made of gold
which was kind of the most important thing
but whatever.

So you know how when you're eating a food you
     really like
and then you get the flu
and you vomit nonstop for like nine whole days
and then suddenly
you do not like that food anymore?
Okay.
So imagine your favorite food is gold
and instead of an upset stomach
your daughter is dead.
Now you understand how Midas feels.
So he turns into a filthy gold-hating hippie
and abandons his entire kingdom
and becomes a follower of this god named Pan
who is a satyr
and is in charge of playing music on some pipes
and Midas gets taught to play music by Orpheus

who I will totally tell you about later
because he is SO SWEET.

So then one day Pan is talking shit about Apollo
the god of guitar riffs and prophecy
and saying how he can totally play better music than
    that guy
so Apollo shows up and is like "Bring it."
and Pan definitely brings it
and Midas is all clapping his hands and singing along
but then Apollo just plays
a SINGLE POWER CHORD
and this power chord is so legit
    that the judge just immediately gives him the win
But Midas is like "Dude, he didn't even play a song.
Try not to choke on that dick, guys."
and Apollo is all "I'LL TEACH YOU TO LISTEN TO
    MUSIC CRITICALLY."
and BAM
Midas suddenly has donkey ears.
He gets super-embarrassed
and hides his ears under a massive turban all the time
but of course his barber knows his secret
because even as a filthy hippie
Midas is too regal to cut his own hair
and he swears the barber to secrecy
but the secret is TOO GREAT AND IMPORTANT
    FOR ONE MAN TO BEAR
so the barber does the only sensible thing
which is to dig a hole in the ground
and whisper the secret into it.
But then a bunch of reeds grow out of the dirt
and start whispering the secret everywhere
like "KING MIDAS HAS DONKEY EARS"
even though it is totally none of their business.
All of which just further proves the old adage:

Mo' money
mo' problems.

✦ ✦ ✦

TIRESIAS IS TWICE
THE MAN/WOMAN
YOU'LL EVER BE

Let me introduce you to the baddest prophet around.
His name is TIRESIAS.

So besides having an awesome name
Tiresias is this guy who was out hiking one day
and he sees these two snakes doing it
and so he just goes "WHAT?
I DON'T WANNA SEE NO SNAKES DOIN' IT UP
    ON THIS MOUNTAIN."
and just runs up and beats them to death
with his trusty walking stick
LIKE A BADASS.

Now that's all well and good
but apparently Hera was REALLY excited
about seeing these snakes do it
because then she gets REALLY pissed
and says "SO YOU LIKE BEATING THE SHIT
    OUT OF SNAKES, HUH?
WELL HOW ABOUT I MAKE YOU
. . . into a woman for some reason."

So bam, Tiresias becomes a woman for seven years.
He doesn't treat it as a punishment basically at all
and in fact he just shits right into Hera's hands
by becoming the best prostitute the world has ever seen.
S/he invents so many new sex positions
that they have to revise gravity to accommodate them.
It is that kind of party.

So after seven years of awesome loveless sex
Tiresias is wandering through the mountains again
and he/she sees two snakes doing it
and just says "Fuck it"
and runs up and beats them to death again
at which point Hera kind of sighs
and realizes that she is not going to teach this
        motherfucker anything about anything
and turns him back into a man
because if you are going around
beating the shit out of reptiles
what are you, if not the ultimate man?

CUT TO A FEW WEEKS LATER.
Zeus and Hera have kind of an argument
which is not unusual for them.
The argument is about who enjoys sex more:
dudes or chicks.
Hera says it's gotta be dudes
presumably because she has never enjoyed sex with her
        awful cheating husband
and Zeus says it's definitely gotta be chicks
presumably because he has a hyperinflated sense of his
        own sexual prowess
so the two of them yell at each other and throw
        lightning for a while
until finally they're like "Wait a second

we totally know a dude who has also been a chick
and has had SCADS of sex as both types.
Maybe we should try asking him?"

So they go hit up Tiresias like "Yo
who has sexier sex, dudes or chicks?"
And Tiresias is like "OH MAN
I thought you would never ask.
Now, I have had some sex in my day
I've played naked Twister and Boner Bingo
and all the different kinds of Yahtzee
but I've gotta say
when it comes to chicks and dudes
I actually figured it out mathematically
and it turns out chicks enjoy sex
exactly NINE TIMES MORE THAN DUDES."
And Zeus is like "HAH!
I TOLD YOU, HERA!
JUST BECAUSE I PUT NO EFFORT INTO OUR
    SEX LIFE
DOES NOT MEAN
THAT YOUR EXPERIENCE IS THE NORM."
And Hera is like "GODS DAMMIT, TIRESIAS
MY HUSBAND DID NOT NEED ANOTHER
    EXCUSE TO NOT TRY IN BED.
LET'S SEE HOW MUCH YOU ENJOY SEX
WITHOUT YOUR EYESSSS."
and Tiresias is like "Well, actually
the eyes are not erogenous zones so . . .
OH SHIT, I'M BLIND NOW."
And Zeus is like "Hera, why you gotta be like that?
Is it because I blackmailed you into marrying me
and now I only bang whores?
Because if so
then there's no reason to take it out on Tiresias.
Yo, T-dawg, I'm sorry about my wife, bro.

Lemme go ahead and give you the gift of prophecy to
    make up for that."
And Tiresias is like "Okay
that works out pretty well actually."
And then after that he shows up in a whole bunch of
    stories
and he is always right about everything he says
and no one ever fucks with him because he is psychic
and also probably a sex god.

So the moral of this story is for the fellas.
Fellas
before you complain
that pleasing your lady is too difficult
try walking a mile in her boobs.

And as long as we're talking about things Tiresias
    did . . .

❖ ❖ ❖

Narcissus Probably
Should Have Just
Learned to Masturbate

So this story begins, like all good stories, with a hot
    nymph.
She's blue
literally, her skin is blue.
That's not really important to the story
I'm just giving you all the facts.

Anyway, one day she's out near some river
and the local river god Cephisus
who no one has ever heard of
is like "Maybe if I rape this nymph
the other gods will take me seriously."
So he half drowns poor Liriope
by encircling her with his winding streams
(wink wink)
and then at that point
she really has nothing to do but get seduced
so they have a kid.
This kid is named Narcissus.

Narcissus is *gorgeous*.
Like, imagine if someone could *look*
exactly like bacon *tastes*
and you have a pretty good picture of Narcissus
(unless you're a vegetarian).
So his mom is like "Oh snap
my skin is BLUE and I STILL got raped.
What the hell is going to happen to my kid?
He's not even a year old and already looks like he could
    suck the red off a fire truck."
So she takes Narcissus to see the baddest
    motherfucker in the land
who is of course Tiresias
And Liriope is like "Is my son going to get raped?"
and Tiresias looks up from his work
which is beating snakes to death with a stick whenever
    they try to get their freak on
And he's like "Bitch, please.
Kid's gonna be fine
just as long as he doesn't
COME TO KNOW HIMSELF."
And Liriope is like "What the hell does that even
    mean?"

And Tiresias is like "QUIET, WOMAN.
I THINK I HEAR SOME SNAKES HAVING
    SEX."
Then he runs off, brandishing his stick.

So Liriope is just like whatever
and Narcissus grows up to be a strapping young lad
so strapping in fact
that by the time he is sixteen
every last person in his town
wants to bang the bajeezus out of him.
But Narcissus is like "Sorry ladies/dudes/centaurs
 I have unreasonably high standards."
So basically, no one is happy.

Then one day
Narcissus goes walking in the forest
where bad shit just generally tends to happen
and this nymph named Echo sees him
and of course, being as this nymph has eyes
she is instantly head over vagina in love with him.
There is a problem though
which is that "Echo"
is not just some kind of playful nickname
it refers to the fact
that she cannot say anything
except for things she has just heard other people say
because Hera got pissed off
about how she used to use her silver tongue
to buy Zeus some precious escape time during his
    adultery runs
and maybe also used her silver tongue on Zeus in other
    ways.
Would that feel good, even?
A silver tongue?
ANYWAY.

So Echo is stalking Narcissus through the woods
not able to say anything
but I guess she makes some kind of noise
'cause then Narcissus is all "WHO'S THERE?"
and Echo is like "WHO'S THERE?"
and Narcissus is like "NARCISSUS"
and Echo is like "NARCISSUS"
and Narcissus is like "YES"
which Echo mistakes for consent
so she jumps out of the woods like "YESSSS"
and comes running toward him, totally nude
and Narcissus is like "Hey, totally naked hot nymph
allow me to introduce you to my unreasonably high
    standards.
Unreasonably high standards, meet naked hot
    nymph."
So Echo runs back into the woods crying
except she probably can't even cry
without hearing someone else do it first
but anyway she gets pretty butthurt about the whole
    thing
and not in the good way that she wanted
so she just mopes around the forest
until her body actually DISAPPEARS
and only her voice remains
and then she uses that voice
to pray to Aphrodite
(or actually Venus
because this is the Roman version of the story)
and is like "Mess this dude up for me, okay?"
I'm not sure how she managed to make up this prayer
    all on her own
but I like to think she probably did it
by hanging around the legions of chicks
who all wished Narcissus was dead because he
    wouldn't bone them.

So Venus hears the prayer and is like DONE
and Narcissus suddenly gets super thirsty
and the only water in the woods
happens to be this deep pool
of crystal-clear springwater
so he starts drinking out of it
but then he stops
because he realizes that what he is drinking
is the face of the most beautiful man he has ever seen.
He falls so in love with this hunk of pubescent glory
that he pines after this dude for like, days
until he realizes
PLOT TWIST
the dude in the pond is actually a reflection
OF NARCISSUS HIMSELF
because apparently
for the last SIXTEEN YEARS OF HIS LIFE
he has NEVER SEEN HIS OWN REFLECTION.
He has never taken a bath
or like, had a cup of water
or, you know, stared REALLY HARD at a bald guy.
He has led a pretty sheltered life, apparently.

So anyway he gets REALLY DEPRESSED
and like, rips off all his clothes
and refuses to eat
which not only makes him more attractive to himself
but also dead
and he goes down to basically the shittiest part of hell
and spends the rest of forever staring at his reflection
    in the river Styx.
Meanwhile, Echo's voice shows up in the woods and
    finds Narcissus's body
and is like "Dammit.
Wish I'd kept my body.
Can't even fondle his corpse now."

And she kind of feels pretty bad about the whole thing
and makes a flower grow out of his corpse
as a kind of a consolation prize for dying.

So from now on
every time you see a narcissus flower
just remember
that if you are beautiful
you should never drink water
because it is too dangerous.

❖ ❖ ❖

Persephone Is the Mother of Invention . . . No, Wait . . .

So Persephone is the daughter of this chick Demeter
who is the goddess of like
fertility and crops and whatnot
and she is also incredibly hot.
So hot, in fact
that Hades is down in the underworld (which is also
    called Hades actually)
and he looks up one day and he sees her and he goes
"DAAAAAAAAAAA
AAAAAA
AAAAA
AAAA
YUM.
I gotta get me some of *that*."

So he just pops on up to the world
in his black chariot of ultimate wretchedness
and he says "Hey, little girl
do you want to come to hell?"
and she probably would have said no
only he kidnapped her.
Basically Hades is the ultimate ladies' man.
So then they're kind of hanging out down in hell
and it's always been pretty depressing in hell
but it's actually a little bit better with Persephone there
because she's not a little emo bitch like Hades is all
    the time
even though he has a WHOLE BADASS KINGDOM
ALL TO HIMSELF.
Seriously, why's he always gotta be moping?
Anyway, Persephone pulls some interior decorating
like some spooky feng shui and shit
and WHAM
hell is a pretty okay place to live all of a sudden.

But all is not well
because meanwhile, Persephone's mom, Demeter, is up
    in the regular world
fretting the shit out of herself over her missing
    daughter
and it does not help at all when she finds out
that she was kidnapped by the king of hell.
So Demeter gets real depressed
and when Demeter gets depressed
all the plants die
and everything freezes
and being alive just kind of starts to suck
because she is the goddess of like
crops and seasons and whatnot.
And see, up to this point
no one has even heard of winter

but now they are getting nothing but winter
nonstop and out of control
24/7/365
except actually maybe only for several months
but either way
shit is intolerable.

So Zeus gets fed up
and he goes and hits Demeter up, and he says
"HEY, BITCH, WHAT'S WITH ALL THE
　　WINTER?"
and Demeter says "Hmm, I dunno.
Maybe it's because your brother is raping my daughter
　　in hell?"
And Zeus says "Hmm, good point."
So he goes down to the underworld
and he says "Listen, bro
I hate to block your cock, but like
shit is completely intolerable up in the real world
and it is downright impossible
for me to get any quality dick laid down
at this ball-freezing temperature.
So give Demeter her daughter back
and don't you dare try any funny business
such as for example
feeding her any food at all from the underworld
because as you know
if she eats any of it
she will be forced to stay in Hades with you forever.
'Cause that's one of those dumb rules you have when
　　you're a god."
And Hades says "Yeah, bro, for sure.
That would be a tragedy.
Nobody wants that."
and then as soon as Zeus is out the door
Hades turns around

all like "'Sup, Persephone?"
and Persephone says "'Sup?"
and Hades is like "Hey, are you hungry?"
and she says "Well, now that you mention it
I haven't eaten or drunk a single thing
since you brought me down here months ago."
(Hades is the consummate host)
So Hades goes "Well, hey
absolutely the only thing we have to eat here in the
    underworld
is POMEGRANATES."
(Which is yet another reason the underworld is
    awesome and Hades should stop whining.)
So he starts feeding her the pomegranate seeds one at
    a time
and he manages to stuff six into her mouth
when her mom shows up
like "Okay, honey
time to go home"
and Persephone says "Okay
I was getting kind of tired of getting raped in hell
    anyway."
and Hades says "HAHAHA PRANK'D
I FED HER SOME FOOD
SHE HAS TO STAY NOW"
And Demeter is like "ZEUUUUSSSS!"
And Zeus is extremely flustered
because he has probably just been interrupted
in the midst of a whole litany of vigorous boning
and he says "OKAY
YOU KNOW WHAT YOU GUYS
JUST . . . JUST FUCKING COMPROMISE
LIKE I KNOW THERE'S A RULE ABOUT THE
    FOOD OR WHATEVER
AND I DONT EVEN KNOW WHY WE HAVE
    THAT RULE HONESTLY

BUT LIKE
I AM LITERALLY FREEZING MY BALLS OFF
    UP HERE
SO HOW ABOUT HADES GETS HER FOR SIX
    MONTHS
AND DEMETER GETS HER FOR THE OTHER
    SIX?"
and Demeter says "Fine
but I'm gonna freeze the shit out of everything for the
    six months my daughter is gone."
and Zeus says "Fine
guess I'm just going to have to double up on the
    amount of banging I do in the summer."
and Hades says "Fine
I guess I'll have to double up on the amount of banging
    I do during the winter."
And it works out in the end
because both Zeus and Hades know
that when either one of them is getting laid
he does not have to ever worry
about thinking about the other one having any sex
and just ruining the mood
because they both know for a fact
that they are never getting laid at the same time ever.
That's how that works.

So the moral of this story
is once again for the gentlemen:
Gentlemen
learn to cook
one home-cooked meal, and BAM
she will be trapped inside of your house forever
or for half the year if she has a good lawyer.

◆ ◆ ◆

HEPHAESTUS GETS DICKED AROUND A LOT

So one of the most inexplicable things about the Greek
    pantheon
is that Aphrodite is married to Hephaestus
Aphrodite is like the high school cheerleader of the
    Greek pantheon
and Hephaestus is the guy with the gimp leg
who is always making historically accurate World War
    II models.
He doesn't actually make World War II models
because World War II has not been invented yet
but he does have a gimp leg
I'm not making that part up.
He got it because when Zeus and Hera first had him
he was SO UGLY
that they actually THREW HIM OFF OF MOUNT
    OLYMPUS
and he fell for seven days
and they only ever let him back up on Olympus
once he showed them that he could make them really
    nice jewelry.
ZEUS AND HERA:
ULTIMATE PARENTING

Look, the point is that Aphrodite is the goddess of
    boning everyone all the time
and Hephaestus is the god of sitting in a forge all day
making armor and swords for all the muscle-y dudes

who go out and murder other muscle-y dudes
and then bone everyone all the time
So why the fuck is Hephaestus married to Aphrodite?
How did he score such sweet tail?
Well, first of all
Hera felt bad about chucking him off a cliff
and her idea of an apology was to GIVE HIM
    APHRODITE.
(Ultimate parenting)
And second of all
Aphrodite is the goddess of boning EVERYONE
ALL THE TIME
so it's not like she's gonna actually be faithful or
    anything
and in fact she is sort of making a habit of boning Ares
the god of war
who is like the quarterback to her slutty cheerleader.
She is actually doing this IN HEPHAESTUS'S BED
when he is out working at the forge
probably making armor for Ares even.
But Hephaestus gets wise to their crafty scheme
mainly because the Sun is a gossipy bitch
and he decides to show his cheating whore of a wife
    what's what
WITH SCIENCE.

So he melts down the armor he was making for Ares
and he uses all the metal to make some chains
and then he uses his mad skills to turn these chains
into a giant indestructible net
that is also invisible somehow
and then he hangs the net over his bed like a canopy
and the next time Aphrodite and Ares hop in there
for a little bit of wango bango
Hephaestus leaps into the room all like
"SURPRISE, BITCH!"

Except he can't leap because he has a gimp leg
but anyway he drops the net on them
and it traps them on his bed
BUT THE JOKE'S ON HIM
because they had no intention of leaving the bed
and they're both like "Welp
we're caught.
Might as well continue our boner fiesta in plain view."
BUT THE JOKE'S ON THEM
because Hephaestus invited all the other gods
to come hang out in his bedroom today.
So they all start rolling in
and Dionysus is laughing his ass off
because he can totally see nipple
and Poseidon pokes Zeus and says "Would you tap
    that?"
and Zeus says "Probably I already have."
(I am not making that up.
That shit is in *The Odyssey*.)
But really the joke is still on Hephaestus
because his wife is boning another man right in front
    of him
and even the best blacksmith cannot repair a broken
    relationship.

✦ ✦ ✦

ORPHEUS ROCKS HARD

Seriously, this dude has all the hookups.
First of all his mom is a Muse
specifically the Muse of singing.

Second of all, when he is like five years old
Apollo shows up at his house
all like, "WHAT UP, ORPHEUS
I AM HERE TO BANG ONE OF YOUR MOM'S
    SISTERS
HEY, DO YOU WANT A LYRE?"
For those of you who don't know
a lyre is basically a kind of ultraharp.
Pretty much how it works
is if Apollo gives you one
then you have a future in the music industry.
So naturally at some point
Orpheus just goes down to Earth
and starts melting face with his amazing music.
Seriously, this shit is fantastic.
It is so fantastic that when this dude Jason is getting
    some Argonauts together
(Argonauts are dudes who go around on a boat called
    the *Argo*)
he is like
"I know we are all seriously bad dudes on this ship
with like muscles and stuff
but you know what we need?
We need a dude with a lyre."
And they get Orpheus.
And then when they sail past the Sirens
who sing such sexy music that any dude who hears it
    drowns himself trying to hit that
Orpheus proceeds to solo SO HARD
that nobody can hear the Sirens
and anyway nobody cares
because Orpheus is wayyyy better than those
    skanks.

So obviously a dude like this is pulling down tail left
    and right

like he's trying on costumes at the Godzilla costume
    warehouse
but his favorite chick is this broad named Eurydice.
I don't know that much about her
but probably she was pretty hot
because, I mean
Orpheus was essentially the ultimate rock star
with, like
additional rock stars taped to each of his fingers.
He had his pick of the crop is what I'm saying.
But Eurydice is none too bright.
because one day
when she and Orpheus are out walking
she steps on a shitload of snakes
and the snakes kill her, obviously.
This is what happens when you step on snakes.
If only Tiresias had been around
this might never have happened.

So Orpheus just sits right down and composes
THE ULTIMATE EMO SYMPHONY.
It is so incredibly drenched in secret pain
that Zeus comes down and is like "Hey, man
I cannot get these chicks in the mood with this Linkin
    Park shit you got goin' on.
Play some Barry Manilow or something, jeez."
But Orpheus says "Sorry, man
I am just way too bummed."
and Zeus says "Okay, crybaby
why don't you just go down to Hades and get your lady
    back, then?"
Orpheus says "I think I will."

So Orpheus goes to Hades
and he just charms the pants off of Hades so hard
with his lyre and his singing

that Hades says
"Fine, dude.
Give me back my pants you just charmed off
and I will give you back your woman
but only if you pass a ludicrous and arbitrary test:
See, your chick's ghost will follow you
all the way out of Hades
but you can't look at her until you're both in the real
    world, or I get her for keepsies.
Make sense?"
and Orpheus says, "Not really, but okay."
And he starts walking.
And on the way out he sees a bunch of demons
So he's like "Hey, demons."
And they're like "'Sup, Orpheus?"
And he says, "Oh, just leading my chick out of hell."
And they say, "Your chick? What chick?"
and then they kind of chuckle a little bit.
So this is making Orpheus nervous
like, REAL nervous
and he really wants to look
but he knows he can't look
so at the VERY MOMENT that he steps out of Hades
he turns around to see if she's really there
and guess what?
SHE IS
but she is STILL IN HELL.
So Orpheus fails the test
and Eurydice disappears forever
and he's back to square motherfuckin' one.
This upsets him so much that he vows to only screw
underaged boys for the rest of his life.
So he goes and sits on a hill
and dyes his hair black
and just plays emo shit all the time

until one day all of these followers of Bacchus show up
and they're like "Hey, dude, we're having a party
right here right now.
You still down with Bacchus?"
and Orpheus is like "Fuck no.
I only worship the SUN."
And they are like "Dude, are you sure about that?
We are a bunch of hot chicks
and we are about to have an orgy
and only people who are down with Bacchus are
    invited to the orgy."
And Orpheus says "Hell no.
I only have sex with people's SONS."
And the chicks are all like, "Well, okay, if you say so"
and then they tear off his skin
and rape his corpse
and rip his head off
and chuck it into a river
along with his lyre
which he is inexplicably still able to play
and he just floats off down the river
making awesome music forever.

So the moral of the story is
Unless you can play your instrument
with your head ripped off
and your arms and skin missing
You Are Not a Real Musician.

◆ ◆ ◆

FRIENDS DON'T LET
FRIENDS BANG COWS

So this dude Minos is having all kinds of problems
    being king of Crete
because his brothers all want to be the king of Crete
    instead
so they are all murdering each other like nonstop
until Minos is like "Hey, Poseidon
you should make me win."
And Poseidon is all "Okay
I am going to send you a bitchin' white bull.
It means you will win
but you have to kill it later in my honor."
And Minos says "Sure, okay, just make me king
    already."
So Poseidon sends this bull
and Minos becomes king
but then he REALLY likes this bull.
I don't think you guys understand
what hot shit bulls were in ancient Greece
you have to remember
Minos didn't have the Internet
so bulls were like
THE HEIGHT OF TECHNOLOGY
and this was like the APPLE IPAD OF BULLS
so he decides "How 'bout I don't kill this bull?
What's the worst that could happen?
I'm already king, right?"
WRONG.

Well, I mean, he is already king
but something bad definitely happens
because Minos has a wife
and Poseidon goes and hits up Aphrodite
like "You know what you should do?
You should make Minos's wife
fall in love with MY BULL."
and Aphrodite looks up from giving Ares a blow job
and she's like "Okay, lemme just finish this."
So all of a sudden
Minos's wife is like *mad* attracted to this cow
but the problem is that the cow is not at all into chicks.
Human chicks, I mean.
It's not a gay cow.
Not that that would have been a problem.
Some of my best friends are gay cows.
But anyway Minos's wife has this brilliant idea
so she calls up this dude Daedalus
and she is like "I need someone to build me a giant
     wooden cow suit
so I can fuck cows"
and Daedalus
who is a fantastic genius inventor
with no concept of right and wrong
is like "Sure, no problem."
And he makes her the suit
and she puts it on
and she goes out and makes hot animal love to that bull
simultaneously inventing furries
and getting totally preggers
and Minos is none the wiser
until she gives birth to a HIDEOUS COWBABY
aka THE MINOTAUR.

So Minos does the smart thing
and calls up the Oracle at Delphi

because that never leads to bad decisions
and the Oracle says "Dude, just build a maze around it.
No harm no foul."
So Minos calls up Daedalus
(the same Daedalus who caused all these problems
    with his excellent cow suit)
and he hires him to build this awesome maze
and then instead of paying him with money
he pays him with years in prison
locked in a tower over the ocean with his son Icarus.
Minos is a dumbass though
because he has locked a master craftsman and his son
in a tower
along with an apparently unlimited supply
of feathers and wax.
So they make wings with that stuff
and jump out the window.

But you know who else is a dumbass?
ICARUS
because he does not understand
that the sun is made of heat
whereas his wings are only made of wax and bird hair
so he flies way the hell up toward the sun
and the sun says "Aw *hell* no"
and Icarus's wings melt and he drowns
and his genius dad lives happily ever after
no longer hampered by his dumbass son
or else he flees all over the country for years trying to
    avoid Minos
before finally convincing someone to murder Minos in
    a bathtub
or maybe both
and then it turns out Daedalus even fucked up the
    labyrinth

because a few weeks later some dick named Theseus
just rolls in and kills the minotaur
and then escapes and gets laid a whole bunch
and then falls off a cliff and dies
but that's a whole other story
and I just told you all the good parts anyway.

So the moral of the story
is don't count your chickens before they hatch
because the chickens might be minotaurs.

NORSE

Holy shit, my friends
this mythos we are coming up on right now
is the cosmological equivalent
of French-kissing a battle-ax.
These myths are rude, crude, and probably radioactive
they play music too loud
and draw disapproving looks from the elderly
they will wake your mother up
in the middle of the night
by driving a Humvee through the armoire.
Seriously
any mythology in which the principal characters
are a suicidal pirate-wizard
and what essentially amounts to a beard with a
    hammer sticking out of it
is the mythology for me
and for you too
once the Norse get through with you.

✦ ✦ ✦

THE NORSE ARE METAL

So you might already know the way the Greeks
     thought the world got made
and also the Romans
because the Romans are goddamn copycatters
and maybe you have listened to some scientists
or some creation scientists
and you know one or two other ways.
Listen
I want you to forget everything you know about
     creation myths
because this myth
is going to BLOW YOUR DICK OFF FROM PURE
     WONDERMENT
and if you do not have a dick
it is going to SEW ONE ON
and then IMMEDIATELY BLOW IT OFF.
Wanna know why?
because it's NORSE MYTHOLOGY TIME.
SHIT YEAH.

So to start out, the world is already pretty badass.
It is just two things:
One is a sea of pure all-devouring fire called Muspell
guarded by a dude named Surt who is just WAITING
to ride out and murder all the gods
and then set the world on fire.
By comparison, the other half of the world is pretty
     lame.

It is just a whole bunch of ice called Niflheim.
But the best part
is that in between Muspell and Niflheim
there is a big-ass trench called Ginnungagap
which is empirically proven
to be the number one funnest thing to say.
Go ahead and say it. I'll wait.

So Ginnungagap is where shit starts to get real
because the cold from Niflheim
bumps up against the heat from Muspell
and causes a bunch of vapor to condense
in Ginnungagap
to create a frost giant
in Ginnungagap
named Ymir
(not Ginnungagap)
Actually, Ymir is more of an ogre than a giant
and he is actually more of a wuss than an ogre
because what is the first thing this guy does?
He goes to sleep
right there
in Ginnungagap.
Sleeping and sweating like a motherfucker.
He sweats so hard
that a man and a woman grow out of his armpit
and then he sweats EVEN HARDER
causing his legs to fuck each other
and have a baby
so then this cow shows up
and starts shooting milk everywhere
and Ymir drinks all of it
'cause there's pretty much no one else to drink it
other than his legbaby and the armpit people.
Then the cow gets bored and starts licking ice

and all of this licking melts away enough ice
to form the shape of a dude
or maybe it is just the same dude who appeared in
    Ymir's armpit.
(Ymir has mastered the fine art of being a neglectful
    father.)
Anyway, this guy's name is Bor.
He marries Bestla, the daughter of some giant.
Maybe the daughter of Ymir, who knows?
Bor is quite a catch because he is the only man in
    existence.
So Bor and Bestla have three kids
Odin, Vili, and Vé.
Really the only one anyone gives a shit about is
    Odin.
He is the ruler of all things, essentially
and he gets his brothers to help him kill Ymir
who is probably still asleep
and has definitely not done anything to deserve being
    murdered
but Odin seems to think
that he has become TOO EVIL
which probably just means that he was snoring
REALLY LOUD.

Whatever the reason, they kill Ymir.
Nice patricide, Odin.
What are you going to do next
further desecrate your grandfather's body
by tearing him apart
and using his limbs as decoration
for a universe you and your brothers are making?
Yes.
This is exactly what Odin and his brothers do.
I mean you gotta give them credit

they use pretty much every part of this dude.
Like, not only do they make his blood into lakes and
     oceans
and his bones into mountains
and skin into earth
and his teeth into tiny rocks
but they use his skull to make the sky
which is such a dumb idea that they have to get some
     cheap slave labor to make it work.
So they go over to Ymir's corpse
which is crawling with maggots at this point
and they are like "Hey, maggots
wanna be a sentient humanoid species?"
And the maggots are like "DO WE?"
So they turn into dwarves
and Odin is like "Great, awesome
how about you repay us by holding up this skull we
     found.
We wanted to make it into the sky
but skulls are not really meant for that.
We'll even name the guys who do it North, South,
     East, and West.
It will be awesome."
And the dwarves are like "Okay, fine."

But listen, guys
just because they have already used Ymir's skull
and skin and bones and teeth and blood
does not mean they are finished defiling his corpse
because the next thing they do
is they chuck his brains into the air
and they become CLOUDS.
Did you think clouds were beautiful fluffy collections
     of water vapor?
WRONG, ASSHOLE.
BRAAAAINS.

Then they make the stars out of all the sparks coming
    out of Muspell
and give all the land along the coast to the giants
I guess to say sorry for murdering Ymir and building a
    world out of his corpse.
But the giants are still pissed
and Odin is like "I need a fort to protect myself from
    all these giants.
What will I build it out of?
Oh, I know
EYEBROWS."
The fort he builds becomes a safe haven for all the
    humans, called Midgard.
Also, they drag Ymir's corpse over Ginnungagap
And Odin makes a place called Asgard
using surprisingly few of Ymir's body parts
and he lives there with his wife, Frigga
and is startlingly faithful to her
and fathers all the other gods, who are called the Aesir.

So the moral of THIS story
is that we need to invent space travel with a quickness
because all of Ymir's body parts
are about to get REAL ripe, REAL fast.

◆ ◆ ◆

THOR GETS HAMMERED

When Odin finally gets done making the world
and settles down to get busy with his wife, Frigga
the first radical dude to get born is named Thor.

Thor is pretty much the baddest motherfucker you
     will ever lay eyes on.
In fact, if you ever laid eyes on him
he would probably walk up to you and DESTROY
     YOUR EYES WITH HIS HAMMER.
Thor's hammer is called Mjolnir
and it was made like so:

So Loki
(the god of being a needless prick all the time)
sneaks up on Thor's wife, Sif, one day
and shaves off all of her hair
like he's one of the guys on *Jackass* or something
and Thor really loves hair, I guess
so he gets SUPER ANGRY
and he chases down Loki and is like "Hey
how about I cut off all your FACE?!"
and Loki is like "But I need my face
for making infuriating smirks with!"
And Thor is like "Well, how about . . .
I just break every bone in your body?"
and Loki is like "No, I need those too.
How 'bout instead
I have the dwarves make your wife some *new* hair?
it will be made of GOLD and it will grow like
     NORMAL HAIR."
and Thor is like "AWESOME."

So Loki goes to these dwarves
like "Guys, I sorta promised Thor that you would make
     his wife the ultimate toupee."
And the dwarves are like "Sure, no problem.
Do you want us to make it out of gold
or DOUBLE GOLD?
We REALLY FUCKING LIKE GOLD because we
     are DWARVES."

Hey, by the way I'm sorry if I'm being racist against
    dwarves
but that is just how dwarves are, okay?
Some of my best friends are dwarves.
Anyway, Loki is like "Regular gold is fine"
and the dwarves are like "Okay, okay
well, how about we also make you a boat
called *Skidbladnir*
which can fit all your friends and all your treasure
and always has wind in the sails
and can be folded up and put in your pocket when not
    in use
and how about we also make Odin a spear
scratch that, an UNSTOPPABLE spear."
and Loki's like "Damn.
All WE ever did for YOU GUYS was make you hold up
    the sky for forever."

So Loki brings all this sweet loot back to the gods
and then he gets this great idea
which is to bet the dwarves that they can't make three
    more EVEN BETTER treasures
FOR FREE.
But he doesn't have much cash on him, so instead he
    just bets them his HEAD.
And these dwarves named Brokk and Eiti take the deal
because it's not like they have to bet anything
    themselves
and they go to the forge
and Brokk pulls out this big-ass boar skin
and he is like "Okay, Eiti.
It is completely crucial
that you crank the bellows *constantly*."
so Eiti starts doin' it
and pretty soon a big-ass fly lands on his hand
and stings the shit out of it

but Eiti does not care.
He is going crazy with that bellows.
and Brokk makes what he was trying to make.
He brings it to Loki and is like "Okay
so we all love boars, right?
But you know what would make a boar even better?
GOLD.
GOLD MAKES EVERYTHING BETTER.
I AM A DWARF AND I COVERED THIS
FUCKING BOAR IN GOLD."
Okay, look, guys, I am just telling the story.
It is not fair to apply our modern conception of racism
to a bygone past, okay?
I forget what the term for that is, but don't do it.
Anyway the filthy dwarves still need to make two
more things
so Brokk decides to cut out the middleman
and just put some gold directly on his forge
and he's like "Hey, Eiti
remember what you did with the boar?
Just do exactly that, because it is totally crucial."
so Eiti starts working the bellows and lo and behold
the same fucking fly shows up
and bites him on his NECK
but Eiti just toughs it out and keeps on pumpin'
and Brokk finishes the thing he was making
and brings it out to Loki
like "Check this gold ring I made.
I call it Draupnir.
But see the thing is, this is just one gold ring.
Do you think that is enough gold?
I don't think that is enough gold
so what I made it do, is every ninth night
it shits out EIGHT IDENTICAL RINGS.
There will be SO MANY RINGS.
I can melt them down for their gold

and use them to make more rings
that drop out MORE RINGS.
I HAVE CREATED INFINITE GOLD.
This is the dream of every dwarf, because we love gold
    so much.
Did you know we invented rings so we could have sex
    with gold?"
Okay, okay, hold on, guys.
If you have any dwarf friends
maybe you should just have them not read this
    myth
if they have read this far it is already too late
we're pretty much done with the gold part
and you have lost a friend.
Anyway, then Brokk puts a big-ass chunk of iron on
    the forge
And Eiti starts pumping that bellows
and then this SAME FUCKING FLY comes back
and bites his eyelids. His EYELIDS.
But Eiti still just keeps on pumping
until blood from the gaping wounds this fly has
    inflicted trickles down into his eye
and he takes one hand off the bellows
to wipe away all the blood
and the bellows stops and everything is RUINED.
It was supposed to be a hammer called Mjolnir
but now it is a hammer called Mjolnir
WITH A KINDA SHORT HANDLE
and Brokk is like "Dang
maybe I won't get Loki's head after all."
But he still bundles up all the shit and takes it to
Asgard because quitting is for pussies.

And in Asgard all the gods are like "HOLY DAMN
YOU MADE A RING
THAT SHITS OUT MORE RINGS.

YOU DO NOT HAVE TO BE A DWARF TO
    APPRECIATE INFINIGOLD.
Oh, and the boar is pretty nice too.
It could use more gold, maybe."
And then Thor is like "Guys, this hammer is so sweet.
It hits anything I throw it at
and then it always comes back to my hand.
I mean the handle is a little bit short
but that doesn't keep it from NEVER MISSING.
Guys, do you REALIZE how many frost giants we can
    kill with this?
This is the best Norse Christmas EVER."
and Brokk is like "Looks like I won the bet, Loki
I am going to dip your head in gold
and then probably fuck it.
That's what I do, because I'm a dwarf."
Look, I lied when I said the gold part was over.
If you had your dwarf friend just keep reading
because you thought the damage was done
then I am really sorry, man
but you need taller friends.
So Loki starts running as fast as he can
but Thor just got that hammer that can hit anything
100 percent of the time
so he just kind of knocks Loki out and brings him back
and Loki is like "WAIT
I promised you my head
but I never promised you the neck it rests on!
So you can't cut it off. HAH."
So Brokk just sews Loki's mouth shut instead
which is probably the best thing for everybody.

So what we have learned today
is that dwarves give the best birthday gifts
so you should try and make up with your dwarf friends
no matter how short they are, or how bad they smell

or how much they keep eyeing your gold earrings
and licking their lips.

But that's not the last wacky plan the gods come up
    with to avoid paying for shit . . .

✦ ✦ ✦

ODIN GETS CONSTRUCTION DISCOUNTS WITH BESTIALITY

So as our story begins
everything is going pretty good
the giants are leaving everyone alone for a minute
and everything is pretty okay
so obviously Odin has to go and fuck it all up
by making a shitty deal with a giant.
He is like "Hey, giant
bet you can't build a wall around my entire city in nine
    months."
And the giant is like "What do I get if I win?"
And Odin is like "Well, I'm kinda cash poor at the
    moment.
How about Freyja?"
(Freyja is the goddess of love and other icky stuff
gifted to the Aesir by a group of identical gods they
    tried to kill one time.
What Odin is doing is called regifting
and it is in poor taste.)
But Freya is way hot, so the giant is like "Sweet, okay."

And Odin is like "Oh, and if you can't finish the wall in
        time, then I get it for free."
And the giant is like "Sure dude, whatever."

Now Odin is pretty confident that there is no way the
        giant can build a wall in time.
I mean, Asgard is pretty much HUGE.
They had to build a six-mile-long feast hall
just to accommodate Thor's LEFT NUT.
So he just sits back
and prepares to have a partially finished wall
TOTALLY FOR FREE.
You don't become a god by being bad with money
that is a fact.

But this plan is about to backfire SO HARD.
The giant and his unreasonably strong horse
are putting up this wall like it's going out of style.
There are still several months to go
and the wall is almost totally finished.
So Odin is like "Oh shit, I might have to pay this giant
for all the work that he's doing.
UNACCEPTABLE."
So he calls up Loki like "LOKI
SOLVE MY PROBLEMS WITH GIANTS."
And Loki is like "What? Why?"
And Odin is like "REMEMBER HOW WE HAVE
        AN OATH OF KINSHIP
THAT MEANS YOU HAVE TO DO WHAT I SAY?"
And Loki is like "Oh yeah.
Why did we do that again?"
And Odin is like "NO TIME FOR QUESTIONS.
STALL THAT GIANT."

So Loki is like "Sheeeeyiiiit.
I'm a pussy. I can't stop a giant.

But WAIT!
I can stop his horse!
WITH MY PUSSY!"
so he turns into a superhot sexalicious girlhorse
with her lady parts all distended and pungent
and the manhorse gets a whiff of that shit
and is like "I AM CALLING A TIME-OUT ON ALL
    THIS WORKING.
A SEX TIME-OUT."
(Feel free to use these in your everyday life.
I know you were all searching desperately
for some way to justify dropping everything
and just having a bunch of sex.
NOW YOU HAVE THAT JUSTIFICATION.)
So then the giant is like "How am I supposed to finish
    this wall without my powerhorse?
I feel like I may have been cheated by Odin
    just now.
I'm going to go yell at him."

So he goes to Odin's room like "ODIN
WHAT DID YOU DO WITH MY HORSE?"
and Odin is like "I dunno what you're talking about.
It was all Loki's idea."
and the giant is like "FUCK THIS
I'M TAKING FREYJA."
and Freyja is like "Who's taking what now?"
because apparently Odin completely forgot to tell her
    about this deal.
So she's like "THORRRR."
and Thor runs into the room like "What?
Oh, you need me to kill a giant?
Yeah, all right."
So he kills the giant
thus once again saving Odin
from the consequences of his shitty actions.

So a couple months later
Loki finally comes back to Asgard
leading the megahorse he seduced
and also another smaller horse
but what this horse lacks in size
it makes up for in TOO MANY LEGS.
Yes sir, this is THE OCTOHORSE.
(aka Sleipnir)
So Odin is like "Oh shit, give me those."
and Loki is like "NUP.
I'm totally giving the ultrahorse to Freyja."
and Odin is like "Can I at least have the octohorse?"
and Loki is like "Only if I don't have to do what you say
    anymore."
and Odin is like "FINE."
and Loki is like "HAHA, I PRANKED YOU
THAT HORSE CAME OUT OF MY HORSE
    VAGINA."
And Odin is like "Ew, ick.
I still want the horse though."

So the moral of the story
is that only a sucker pays full price for masonry.

Oh, speaking of which
let me tell you about another really gross thing Loki
    had sex with . . .

✦ ✦ ✦

Fenrir Is a DILF

So one day, Loki's wandering around Jotunheim
and he sees this chick Angrboða
pronounced ANGER BOW THE
and he is like "Well, I know she's pretty ugly
and her name is kinda like a reference book entry for
     THE ANGER BOW
but you know what?
I'm gonna tap that
and have three kids with that
and all three of those kids are going to be horrible
     beasts that bring on the apocalypse.
I see no problems with this."

So for now, let's just focus on the first kid:
a giant wolf named Fenrir.
Now Loki brings baby Fenrir to Asgard
and the Aesir all instantly know that this wolf is gonna
     be the death of them
mainly because it is a GIANT WOLF NAMED
     FENRIR.
But instead of doing anything about it
they decide to see if they can just raise it as their own
presumably because they don't want to hurt Loki's
     feelings.
So this god Tyr
the god of single combat and being awesome
gets put in charge of feeding Fenrir

because he's the only person with sufficient testicular
    mass to actually go near the wolf
and Fenrir gets bigger
and bigger
and holy shit bigger
until the gods start to be like "Uhh . . .
we should really do something about this wolf."
So what they do is they make a big metal chain.
This chain is so incredibly massive
that they don't feel right until they give it a name
that name is Leyding.
So they go up to Fenrir like "Hey, man
I bet you totally can't break out of this chain."
And Fenrir is like "Okay, bring it."
So they tie him up
and he pretty much just breaks the chains like cobwebs
and he gets famous because of that
and the gods are like "Fuck, that backfired.
Okay, let's make a better chain."
so they make a chain
that is TWO TIMES AS STRONG
and they name it Dromi
and they go back to Fenrir
like "Bet you can't break THIS chain."
And Fenrir is like "I don't know if I want to let you tie
    me up again."
And the gods are like "Don't you want to be double
    famous?"
and Fenrir is like "Ugh, okay."

So he lets them tie him up again
and he flexes a little, but the chain doesn't break
so then he kicks the chain, and it does break
and the gods are all like "Okay
we definitely need a better chain.
Somebody call some dwarves."

So the dwarves are like "Okay
the mistake you guys have been making
is you have been trying to make a chain
out of actual things that exist
such as metal
instead of abstract concepts
such as the sound of a cat's footfall."
So what the dwarves do
is they take the sound of a cat's footfall
along with the roots of a mountain
the sinews of a bear
the beard of a woman—
remember, these are dwarves—
and the breath of a fish, and the spit of a bird
so that's why you can't hear cats walking around
and mountains don't have roots
and fish don't breathe, and birds don't spit
but I think bears still probably have sinews
and I have definitely met me some bearded ladies
so I guess the dwarves were not that thorough.

But anyway
somehow they manage to distill all this shit into THE
    ULTIMATE CHAIN.
Except it's not a chain, it's a ribbon called Gleipnir.
It is thin and pink and soft
and the gods go and bring it to Fenrir
and are like "Bet you can't get out of this ribbon."
And Fenrir is like "Come ON, guys.
There is no fame to be gained from breaking a little
    girl's pretty, pretty princess bow.
Plus, this is OBVIOUSLY a trap."
And the gods are like "A trap? Whaaaat?
Why would we trap you?
What do you think we are
desperately afraid of you or something?

We just thought
that if the great wolf Fenrir
was too much of a pussnexus
to let himself get tied up by a pretty pink ribbon
we might just go and tell everybody about that
and then they would laugh at you."
So Fenrir is like "OKAY FINE.
But I seriously don't trust you guys
so how about I let you tie me up
if one of you puts your hand in my mouth as collateral."
And all the gods are like "Um . . . well . . ."
Until Tyr is like "I'll do it."
Because Tyr is a FUCKING BADASS
moved almost to the point of vomiting
but what tremendous wusses all his friends are.

So then they tie Fenrir up
and Fenrir flexes
and then he tries kicking
and then he tries flailing around like a fucking lunatic
but that ribbon does not break
and he is like "DAMMIT."
And bites off Tyr's hand
and everyone laughs at Fenrir
except for Tyr
because he just got his hand bit off.
And Fenrir is all trying to scream and bite everyone
so they jam a sword in his mouth to keep it open forever
and Fenrir drools so much
that it makes an entire fucking river
called "hope" in Norse for some reason
like this is some kind of fucked up morbid
    motivational poster.
HOPE:
YOU WILL EVENTUALLY ESCAPE YOUR
    HELLISH PRISON

AND RAIN DEATH AND FIRE UPON
    MIDGARD.
Because actually that is what the Norse prophecy says.
It says that eventually, at the end of the world
Fenrir will get loose and eat Odin.

So I guess the moral of the story
is that if your friend keeps bringing home his mutant
    babies
it is not your responsibility to raise those babies.

Remember this.

◆ ◆ ◆

SEX 4 GOLD

Before we go any further
I feel like I need to tell you
a little bit about the kind of person Freyja is.
But it is difficult to find a myth about Freyja
in which her main role
isn't just as something people give each other.
This is because the Norse appear to treat women as
    currency.
But don't worry, guys
I found one
(kinda)

So Freyja wakes up one morning
and she is like "I JUST HAD A WET DREAM
ABOUT SOME GOLD

AND NOW I WANT SOME.
But where shall I get some?
Oh wait
I live in a world that has dwarves.
WHAT A STUPID QUESTION."

So she walks over to Dwarftowne
and while she is walking, Loki sees her and he is like
"Oh man
that chick looks like she is about to get some
    TREASURE
I want to RUIN THAT ACCOMPLISHMENT
    FOR HER
because I am Loki and that is what I DO."

So Loki follows Freyja
all the way to the house of these four dwarves
and sitting on their pedestal
is just the most astonishing display of golduggery
EVER.
(Golduggery is exactly like skulduggery
except instead of doing crimes you do gold)
It is a necklace of such INDESCRIBABLE VALUE
that all the Norse scribes purposefully lost most of the
    text of this myth
and no one actually knows what it looks like
or even if it is a necklace really
we're kind of just guessing here
more or less based on the fact
that a necklace is the only form of gold
big enough to fit four dwarf dicks simultaneously.

So these four skeezy dwarfs pop out, and Freyja's like
"Ew, gross
I mean hey, guys, how's it going?
Think I could have this necklace or whatever it is?

I'll pay you GOLD for it."
And the dwarves are like
"We don't need any more gold."
WHOA, RECORD SCRATCH.
Did you just hear what I heard?
DWARVES
do not need more
GOLD?!
These are clearly not four dwarves
but rather eight babies in four dwarf suits.
But that just makes this next part weirder
because then Freyja is like
"Well, gold is pretty much all I have.
Credit cards haven't been invented yet, nor has
    investment banking."
and the dwarves are like "WELL
YOU HAVE A VAGINA, RIGHT?
HOWSABOUT WE ALL USE THAT FOR LIKE
    TWENTY-FOUR HOURS APIECE."
and Freyja is like "Hmm
. . .
Okay!"

So each of the dwarves does the teenie-weenie with
    Freyja for a solid day/night cycle
and they are very civil about it
and no one minds getting sloppy seconds
and at the end of the four days the dwarves are like
"Welp
we're about as sexually satisfied as we are ever going to
    be in our sad, sad lives.
Here, have this necklace."
And Freyja is like "SWEET!
This was ALMOST worth debasing myself in this
    manner!"
And meanwhile, Loki

who, remember, followed Freyja here
is like "DAMN, I WISH I HAD FILMED THAT.
I BET THERE'S A WHOLE INTERNET FETISH
    ABOUT THIS KIND OF SHIT.
I guess I'll just have to settle for ruining her
    accomplishment like I planned."

So Freyja goes home to enjoy her necklace
and take a looooong shower
and Loki hauls ass over to Odin's place
and he's like "Odin, Odin, guess what?
I know I'm the god of lying all the time
but you gotta trust me when I say
Freyja just fucked four dwarves for a necklace."
And Odin is like "Yeah, that sounds like Freyja.
I mean WHAT??
I WANTED TO FUCK FREYJA.
WE *ALL* WANTED TO FUCK FREYJA.
THAT'S LIKE THE WHOLE REASON WE KEEP
    HER AROUND
AND ALL WE HAD TO DO ALL THESE YEARS
WAS OFFER HER JEWELRY?
UNACCEPTABLE.
GO STEAL HER NECKLACE."
and Loki is like "Did somebody say STEALING?"
and Odin is like "Yes, Loki, that was me who said that."
but Loki doesn't hear him
because he is already at Freyja's place
STEALING.

So he gets to Freyja's place and the door is locked
so he turns into a fly
and goes in through a crack in the roof.
But then Freyja is sleeping on her back
with the clasp of her necklace completely inaccessible

so Loki turns into a flea
and mauls her cheeks until she flips over
and then Loki turns into Loki
and just steals her necklace.

So Freyja wakes up
notices her necklace is gone
notices her door is open
and is like "DAMMIT LOKI.
But wait
Loki would be too much of a pussy to do this on
    his own.
DAMMIT ODIN.
But how would Odin know about my necklace?
DAMMIT LOKI.
But Loki is probably nine countries away at this
    point.
I'M GONNA GO YELL AT ODIN."

So she shows up at Odin's place, all angry and shit
and Odin is like "WELL, WELL, WELL
IF IT ISN'T SLUT CITY.
HEY, I HAVE SOME BRASS PLATES AND A
    SHINY ROCK.
WANNA GIVE ME A RIMJOB OR SOMETHING?
THEY'RE ALL YOURS."
And Freyja is like "VERY FUNNY ASSHOLE."
and Odin is like "I BET YOU WON'T THINK MY
    ASSHOLE IS VERY FUNNY
WHEN YOU ARE GIVING ME A RIMJOB.
But seriously, it's because of shit like this that we keep
    trying to sell you to giants.
So I'm going to punish you."
and Freyja is like "Aw Frigg.
What's it gonna be?"

And Odin is like "Well, I'll let you have the necklace back
but only if you make all the races of men in Midgard
fight wars forever.
Oh wait, that's not really a puni—"
AND FREYJA IS LIKE "YES, DONE, THANK
    YOU."
Then there is war forever
but at least Freyja looks pretty.

So the moral of the story
is that apparently women ARE currency
but the exchange rate of women to gold
isn't actually that great.

✦ ✦ ✦

THOR GETS JACKED

So Thor's sleeping one night
prolly dreaming about lightning and murder
and he wakes up like "Man, that was a good dream.
'Bout to go make it a reality with the help of my trusty
OH SHIT
WHERE IS MY HAMMER??
LOOOOKIIII"
and Loki shows up like "I didn't do it.
I mean . . . Hey, Thor, what's good?"
And Thor's like
"SOMEONE STOLE MY HAMMER."
And Loki is like "Wow. I actually seriously am not
    responsible for once.
Here, dude, let me help you find it."

So they go see Freyja
and Freyja is like "Hey, Thor, what's good?"
And Thor is like
"SOMEONE STOLE MY HAMMER.
WAAAAHHHH."
and Freya is like "Shut the fuck up, man.
We can solve this mystery.
Loki, did you steal the hammer?"
And Loki is like "Nope."
And Freyja is like "Well, I'm out of ideas."
and Loki is like "I know, right?
But how about this:
how about you lend me your cloak of feathers
that lets you fly
so I can fly over to the land of the giants
and ask them where they hid Thor's hammer
because as you know
if it wasn't me, it was definitely the giants."

And Freyja is like "Sure, man
take my super valuable cloak."
So Loki takes it
and COMPLETELY FAILS TO STEAL IT
all the way to Jotunheim.
and he glides right up to some really rich giant named
    Thrym
who is just sitting up on a mountain
with some hounds on gold leashes
and he is like "Yo, Loki, my man, what's good?"
and Loki is like "You didn't happen to steal Mjolnir,
    did you?"
and Thrym is like "HAHA, YOU GOT ME
I STOLE IT AND THEN I BURIED IT
AND I'LL NEVER GIVE IT BACK
UNLESS I GET TO MARRY FREYJA
HAHAHAHAHAHAHAHAHA."

So Loki flies back to Freyja and Thor
who are both like "HOLY SHIT, LOKI
Did you forget to steal that cloak or something?
It's like you're suddenly respecting people's
    possessions. It's creepy."
And Loki is like "I KNOW, RIGHT?
Look, I can get Mjolnir back super easy.
Here, Freyja, just put on this wedding dress
and Freyja is just like "HELLLLLLLL
NO.
What do you think I am
some kind of slut who trades sex for treasure?
Make Thor do it."
And Thor is like "NOOOOOOOO WAY, JOSÉ.
What do I look like
some kind of cross-dressing motherfucker?
Bitch you could not find a vagina on me if you CUT
    ONE INTO MY FLESH.
SHIT WOULD GROW BACK.
I AM A VIRILE DYNAMO WITH THE HEALING
    POWERS OF WOLVERINE."
and Freyja is like "Yes, Thor, we all understand.
But if you don't get that hammer back
who is going to kill all the giants?
Those giants are going to remain woefully unkilled."
And Thor is like "Fine, I'll put on the dress."

So they pull out ALL the fucking stops
this is like *Pimp My Ride* for drag queens right here.
They give him a veil and a dress
and Freyja's pretty necklace and some house keys
'cause apparently
there is some Norse wedding tradition
where they lock you out of a house
and you have to get inside or else you're divorced
and Thor just feels SOOOO PRETTY

but he won't let anyone know
'cause he's Thor, all right?

And then Loki gets jealous of how pretty Thor is
and is like "I wanna dress up too."
And Freyja is like "All right.
You can be her—I mean HIS wingman or whatever."
Hey, is there a female version of wingman?
Wingwoman sounds awkward.
I'm coining a new phrase:
Titcaptain.
Tell your friends.

So Loki and Thor show up at Thrym's place
and Thrym makes the colossal mistake
of inviting Thor to have dinner with him
so Thor eats an entire ox, and then eight salmon
and all the little cakes and shit they can bring him
and chugs a ton of mead
until Thrym is like "Whoa, baby.
Might wanna slow down there."
And Loki is like "No, man, it's totally cool.
She hasn't eaten in EIGHT DAYS
'cause she was SO EXCITED ABOUT YOUR DICK."
So Thrym is like "Oh okay."
But then he's like "Man
I really wanna kiss my bride right now"
so he lifts up her delicate veil and WHAT THE FUCK
    IS THIS?

Here come Thor's furious eyeballs, flaming with pure
    black hatred
and that is NOT what Thrym was looking for
and he is like "MY, WHAT BIG EYES YOU HAVE"
and Loki is like "No, man, it's fine.
She just hasn't slept for the last eight days

'cause she was so excited about your dick, like I said.
Honestly I don't know how she's even alive
except for the whole immortality thing, I guess."

So then this random chick busts into the room
one of Thrym's daughters or something
and is like "FREYJA, GIVE ME A WEDDING GIFT
EVEN THOUGH I AM NOT GETTING
    MARRIED.
GIVE ME RINGS OF RED GOLD."
and Thor is like "Fuck your red gold.
What do I look like, some kind of red dwarf?
Hey, Thrym, I want a wedding gift actually.
I want Mjolnir."
and Thrym is like "ANYTHING YOU SAY, HONEY."
and goes and digs up Mjolnir and gives it to Thor
and Thor is like "OH, IT IS PARTY TIME NOW,
    MOTHERFUCKERS."

So he kills Thrym
and then all of Thrym's dudes
and then that chick who asked him for gold, just for
    good measure
and then he's like "WHO'S THE MAN?
WHO'S THE MAN?
ME RIGHT?
'CAUSE THIS WHOLE THING KINDA MADE
    ME QUESTION MY SEXUALITY."

So the moral of the story is
if at first you don't succeed
try cross-dressing.

◆ ◆ ◆

ALL'S WELL THAT
MIMIR'S WELL

Odin is constantly doing weird shit for secrets.
Like every morning, he sends out his two ravens—
    Hugin and Munin—to go fly around
and then in the evening
they come back and tell him what's up.

But DISASTER STRIKES
because one day
instead of telling him all the shit they saw
all the birds will say is "OHH SHIT. GOT SOME
    FOREBODING SHADOWS UP IN THIS
    BITCH."
And Odin is like "FOREBODING SHADOWS?
THOSE ARE THE WORST KIND OF
    SHADOWS!"
At which point his wife, Frigga, busts in like
    "HUSBAND, STOP YELLING"
and Odin is like "HOW AM I SUPPOSED TO STOP
    YELLING
WHEN THERE ARE FOREBODING SHADOWS
GOING ON ALL OVER THE PLACE??"
And Frigga is like "Okay, tell you what
how about we go hit up these chicks called the Norns
who live at the bottom of Yggdrassil—
THE TREE OF LIFE—
and look into their eyes for a bit and see the future?"
And Odin is like "Okay, I GUESS."

So Odin gets all his buddies together
them being Tyr, the one-armed badass murder
    convention
Baldur
the prettiest and best loved of all the gods
and Thor, who has a hammer.
They all walk over to this fabulous rainbow bridge
that connects Asgard to the base of Yggdrassil
and Odin goes up to Heimdall
who is the keeper of the gate of Asgard
and also has a sweet gold grill
and Heimdall opens up the gate
and Odin walks through, and Tyr walks through, and
    Baldur walks through
and Thor tries to walk through and Heimdall is like
"NOPE, NO THORS ALLOWED."
and Thor
who is the god of getting real pissed real fast
is all "DON'T MAKE ME COME OVER TO YOUR
    HOUSE AND BEAT YOUR WIFE.
OH WAIT, YOU DON'T HAVE A WIFE
SO I GUESS I AM GOING TO HAVE TO WAIT
UNTIL SOME POOR SKANK FINDS YOUR
    WEAK-ASS GOLD GRILL ALLURING
AND THEN WHEN YOU ARE CUTTING THE
    CAKE AT YOUR WEDDING
I WILL BUST OUT OF THE CAKE
AND CLOCK YOUR NEW WIFE IN THE JAW
    WITH MY HAMMER
BECAUSE IF THERE IS ONE THING
THAT DEFINES ME AS A PERSON
IT IS MY MASSIVE FUCKING HAMMER."
And Heimdall is like "Actually your hammer is kind of
    the problem
the weight of your hammer
combined with the weight of your fat, fat ass

would break the rainbow bridge.
So I'm sorry, dude
but you're going to have to stay home.
UNLESS you want to wade across these two
    smothering miserable cloud rivers
and meet your bros on the other side."
and Thor is like "SOUNDS AWESOME."

So nine hours later, Thor finally catches up to everyone
    at the base of Yggdrassil
and then Odin goes over to stare at the Norns for a bit.
There are three Norns:
Urda, the old one
Verdandi, the hot one
and Skulda, the emo one
and in their eyes Odin can see the future
and I dunno exactly what it is
but it's apparently pretty depressing
and then Frigga shows up
with Sif (Thor's wife)
and Nanna (Baldur's wife. Lucky bitch)
and she looks at the Norns for a bit
and then looks real sad at Baldur, who is her son
presumably because she saw him die in the future or
    some shit.
Who knows?
(Spoiler alert: He totally dies.)

So Odin turns around like "Hey, guys
I need to go to Midgard for a bit.
I need to drink from the well of Mimir
because it is fortified with wisdom and shit
and all these foreboding shadows are going wayyy
    over my head."
And then Thor has to figure out how to get back
    home.

So Odin trades in his spear, and all his armor
and his eight-legged horse, and his name
for a blue cloak and a staff and a big floppy hat
and the name VEGTAM THE WANDERER
and he starts walking through Jotunheim
looking for giants.

Pretty soon he sees him a giant
So he walks up to this giant like "Hey, bro, what's your
    name?"
and the giant is like "I AM VAFTHRUDNIR
WISEST GIANT EVER."
Odin has heard about this dude
and he knows that he is not bullshitting
so he is like "Oh damn, I am in luck.
Wanna hook me up with some wisdom?"
and Vafthrudnir is like "OKAY, BUT FIRST
ANSWER SOME RANDOM TRIVIA
AND IF YOU ANSWER WRONG
I GET TO CUT OFF YOUR HEAD."
This may seem strange
but actually this is just how they play trivial pursuit in
    Sweden.

So Vafthrudnir tosses out a bunch of questions
but his quiz is actually super weak sauce
because like 100 percent of the answers
can be readily found on Wikipedia
so Odin proceeds to hand him his ass
and Vafthrudnir is like "Aww dang.
Now you gotta ask ME a question."
and Odin is like "How about this one:
WHAT ARE THE LAST WORDS THAT ODIN
    WILL SAY TO HIS SON BALDUR?"
And Vafthrudnir is like "COME ON, THAT IS
    ENTIRELY UNFAIR

ONLY ODIN WOULD KNOW THE ANSWER TO—
Waaait a second.
You're Odin, aren't you?
You motherfucker.
Okay, what kind of wisdom did you want to get hooked
    up with?"
And Odin is like "I just wanna know how much it costs
to drink from Mimir's well."
and Vafthrudnir is like "Oh damn, is that all?
You probably could have just asked Mimir.
He generally just charges people THEIR RIGHT
    EYE."
And Odin is like "Really?"
And Vafthrudnir is like "Yup."
And Odin is like "Does he ever charge . . .
anything else?"
And Vafthrudnir is like "Nope."

So Odin is like "Fuuuuck, man
I need my right eye
for like, depth perception
and keeping bacteria out of my bleeding eye socket.
Maybe I shouldn't go through with this."
But then he remembers that he's not a huge wuss
so he goes to Mimir's well
and he's like "Hey, Mimir
hook it up."
And Mimir looks at him and is like
"You know how much it costs, right?
'Cause a lot of people show up here like
'GIMME SOME WISDOM'
and I'm always like 'Sure. One eyeball, please.'
And they are like 'NOOOO WAYYYY.'
I mean, I know you're not gonna pussy out
because I drink from this wisdom well all the time
and I'm wise as shit

but I still gotta ask for legal reasons:
You down to give me your right eye?"
and Odin is like "OH HELLS YES."

So Mimir gives him the water of knowledge right away
which strikes me as an incredibly unwise move
because Odin could have just drunk all the water
and then left without giving away any of his eyeballs
and in fact if that water had really given him ultimate
    wisdom
that's probably exactly what he would have done.
But no, he drinks the water
and he sees what he has to do
to mitigate the horrible foreboding shadow
not that it can be stopped or anything
because Norse mythology is pretty gloomy
and then he puts down the drinking horn
and he plucks out his eye
and he puts his still-warm bleeding eyeball
in Mimir's well
proving once and for all
that the Norse may not have been a very smart people
or a very happy people
but no matter what
THEY WERE ALWAYS METAL.

✦ ✦ ✦

THE END OF THE NORSE
WORLD AS WE KNOW IT

Bad news, guys. In this myth all the Norse gods die.
Yeah, this is the big one:
RAGNAROK
THE END OF THE GODDAMN WORLD.
So basically the first thing that's gonna tip everyone off
that the world is ending
is this thing called Fimbulvetr
which just means THE WINTER OF WINTERS
and that is exactly what it is.
It is a winter
MADE OF MULTIPLE WINTERS
like, there is going to be a winter
and then once that winter is finished
there will be ANOTHER WINTER.
And then after that maybe it will be spring?
Think again, son.
MORE WINTER.

The whole point of this endless winter
is just to put everyone in a really bad mood
to prepare them for the next stage of the apocalypse
which is CEASELESS WARS.
Which is funny
because that is also the Norse idea of heaven.
Like, that is seriously what everyone is doing in
    Valhalla all the time.
But then finally after that goes on for a while

this wolf Skoll
who is one of the sons of Fenrir
is gonna eat the sun.
Then Fenrir's other kid, Hati, will eat the moon,
because he's a fucking copydog.
Then the cock Fjalar will crow to the giants
all like "TIME FOR WAR, MOTHERFUCKERS"
and the golden cock Gullinkambi
will yell the same thing at the gods
and then a third cock will raise the dead.
Hehe, cock.
THEN
there's gonna be A WHOLE BUNCH OF
    EARTHQUAKES
and this is going to have the effect
of finally releasing that evil wolf bastard
Fenrir
and his bottom jaw is gonna touch the earth
and his top jaw is gonna touch the sky
and his eyes are going to be on FIRE
and there's gonna be a whole bunch of tsunamis and
    shit too
because the Midgard serpent, who holds up the world
(and is also another one of Loki's horrible children)
is going to start having seizures all over the ocean
on its way to fuck up the land.
And not only that
but he's going to breathe poison all over everything
constantly
completely destroying all the air
and all the land.
And all the waves caused by the serpent
are gonna set free this ship called Naglfar
full of giants
who are ready to romp and stomp everyone
and another ship is gonna set sail from hell

with all the dead people on it
and Loki is gonna be driving it
because the gods sure as shit want nothing to do with
    him at this point
and guess who else is coming to the party?
FIRE GIANTS.
What are fire giants you ask?
Oh, I don't know, maybe giants MADE OF FIRE
the sole purpose of whom is to show up
at this EXACT MOMENT
led by this guy SURT
and fucking set fire to EVERYTHING.

So this is when Heimdall is going to blow his horn
signaling that SHIT is finally about to get REAL
and Odin and all the other gods
and all the elves, dwarves, demons
and basically just anything ever
are going to ride onto this one battlefield called Vigrid
which means BATTLESHAKER
and they are going to tear each other to pieces
in the following order:
Odin is going to fight Fenrir
and Fenrir is going to eat Odin
and then Odin's son Vidar is gonna be like "NOOOO."
and run up and rip Fenrir's jaw in half
which is pretty appropriate
because Vidar is the god of revenge
not that he has anything to really be vengeful about
because Odin is EVERYONE'S dad.
Meanwhile, Thor is gonna fight the Midgard serpent
and he is gonna kill it
but then its poison is gonna kill HIM.
And Surt is just gonna pick the weakest-looking god
Freyr
who is the god of the sun and elves and shit

and just kill him straight up
because Freyr is a tremendous pussy
who actually FORGOT TO BRING A SWORD
TO THE APOCALYPSE.
Then Tyr is gonna look around like "Shit
I need to kill someone to prove I'm a badass.
How about this terrible wolf, GARM?!"
and he kills it, despite the fact he only has one hand
but then Garm also kills him. Boo.
Also, Heimdall kills Loki, FINALLY
but Loki also kills Heimdall, so that will suck.
And on top of ALL OF THAT
Surt is gonna just start chucking fire in every direction
burning everything
so it won't even really matter if you survive the epic
    battle
because everyone is catching fire anyway
except for these two people
Lif and Lifthrasir
a dude and a chick who will just be sleeping
in the indestructible forest.
Wait, there's an INDESTRUCTIBLE FOREST??
Why doesn't everyone just evacuate there?
That would seriously minimize some casualties.

Anyway, when it's all over
and the earth dives underwater to try and put out all
    the fire
and then comes back up again all fresh and new
Lif and Lifthrasir are gonna repopulate the world
and everything is going to be great forever.

So the moral of the story
is that when the going gets tough
the tough get going
but the SMART get inside the invincible forest.

EGYPTIAN

You might not guess from their tame 2-D cave
     paintings
but the ancient Egyptians
liked to tell some seriously messed-up myths
they've got all the essentials:
booze, blood, and jerkin' it
(if you thought that the essentials were food, water,
     and shelter
then you, my friend
have been reading the wrong myths)
and if any mortals actually managed to survive
the constant barrage of nonsense from above
Egyptian lore says you had to get your soul weighed
against a FUCKING FEATHER
by a pitiless demon with a dog for a head
and if your soul is heavier than the feather
YOU GO TO HELL.
So I hope you can hear me in hell, every dude who ever
     lived in ancient Egypt
because I am about to seriously bastardize your canon
     up in here.

♦ ♦ ♦

Ra Has Sex with Himself

So there is this dude named Ra.

This dude does not exist
At least not at the beginning of the story.
All there is is this totally boring infinite water
called Nu
but then Ra
who—remember—doesn't exist
is like "This sucks.
How about I CREATE MYSELF USING PURE
    WILLPOWER!??"
So now Ra is standing around
except actually he is not standing.
He hasn't invented standing yet
and anyway there is no place to stand
so Ra is like "Okay, time for some terrain features.
Let's start with the ones that look the most like tits."
So he makes a hill
and he stands on it
and later someone builds a temple BUT LET'S NOT
    GET AHEAD OF OURSELVES.

So Ra gets pretty bored
seeing as all there is in the ENTIRE GODDAMN
    UNIVERSE is a hill and some water.
So he hangs out on the hill for a bit
waiting for other awesome dudes to will themselves
    into being

but they don't
so he's like "MAN, YOU GUYS ARE SOOOO LAZY
FINE, I'LL MAKE MY OWN FRIENDS."
But there is a problem
because, although Ra can make hills
and also HIMSELF
he apparently can't make people.
Sexual reproduction is ruining everything, as usual.
But Ra does not even give a shit
he just goes right ahead and FUCKS HIS OWN
        SHADOW UNTIL HE GETS PREGNANT.
THEN HE GIVES BIRTH TO KIDS
OUT OF HIS MOUTH
IN THE TWO LEAST CLASSY WAYS POSSIBLE.
Yes, guys.
If Egypt is to be believed
you are all either descended from spit or puke
(depending on whether you are a boy or a girl).

See, Ra has two kids.
The phlegm kid is this dude called Shu
the god of air and stuff
meanwhile the vomit kid is a chick named Tefnut
goddess of moisture
not water mind you, but moisture
which makes sense with the whole vomit thing, I guess.
Anyway, Shu and Tefnut get together
and by their powers combined
manage to be exponentially more bored
than even their omnipotent father could have imagined.
So they are sitting around and they are like "Hey
wanna hit each other with bricks?
Oh wait, bricks don't exist.
Just like absolutely everything else other than hills.
Fuck it, let's make up some codes of laws and then get
        lost."

So they make up some laws and then they get lost
in the middle of an endless ocean fiasco
which is kind of like SeaWorld
if SeaWorld was everything everywhere
and there was no Shamu
and there was no amusement park
or hot dogs or whatever.
It is actually just the water part of SeaWorld.
And there are only three people there
and two of them are lost
and they are made of spit and vomit.
Actually, that last part sounds a lot like SeaWorld.

So Ra is like "GUYYSSSS
I fucked my own SHADOW so I wouldn't be lonely.
Come baaaack."
And then he takes out his one eye
(by the way, he only has one eye)
and he is like "Hey, eye
go find my kids."
So it does, and it brings them back to Ra
and he starts crying
either because he is so happy to have his kids back
or because now he has to raise kids
but the myth is not clear on whether he puts his eye
        back in before he does this
or whether it is just this weird floating sadness orb
but that is not important at all.
What is important
is that those tears hit the hill Ra made
and they turn into people
and then Shu and Tefnut start boning
like siblings do.
They pop out this kid Geb, the earth
and Nut, the sky
(those are extremely large babies, no lie).

Then later, Geb and Nut give birth to all the trendy gods
like Isis and Osiris and whatever
and things proceed pretty much as would be expected
with a lot of murder and sex and stuff.

So basically what it all comes down to
is that we are made of tears
from the disembodied eyeball
of a guy who fucks his own shadow
and surrounds himself with spit and puke.
I'm gonna go cry now.
I hope it doesn't turn it into babies.

$$\blacklozenge \; \blacklozenge \; \blacklozenge$$

Ra and Sekhmet, or:
How Beer Saved
the Universe

So Ra creates the world.

Sure, great
but just because you create the world
doesn't mean you get to just be king of it forever.
I mean you get to be king of it for a *while*
(like for example what Ra does
is as soon as he's done creating everything
he turns into a dude and becomes king of Egypt)
but the problem with dudes is that they get old
and the problem with old dudes
is that they are constantly getting guff

from ALL DIRECTIONS
and the problem with being a god
is that you are constitutionally incapable
of taking ANY GUFF WHATSOEVER
so naturally
when everybody starts laughing at Ra's old hair and
    senility
he gets *real* pissed
and when you are a god
and you are real pissed
there is only one solution, my friends:
GENOCIDE.

So basically what Ra does
is he turns around and gives Egypt the world's
    DEADLIEST STINKEYE
this eye is so stinky
it produces an entire brand new goddess
the goddess is named Sekhmet
and she is basically like a lioness
with *chainsaws for legs*
SEKHMET:
THE ORIGINAL THUNDERCAT.

Sekhmet's job is simple:
KILL.
EVERYONE.
So that is what she does.
She just tears all around everywhere
mauling the ever-loving crap out of people
until the ground is like
permanent red
which is disconcertingly tacky.
Eventually Ra wakes up from his old-man sleep
and he's like "WHOA
WHERE DID ALL THE PEOPLE GO?

Damn, I feel kinda bad now."
Gods are always doing things like this
if you haven't noticed.
But the problem is that by now Sekhmet is an
    unstoppable murder engine.

But the good news
is that there is ONE THING
with the power to stop an unstoppable murder engine
and that thing
is BOOZE.

So what Ra does
is he gathers up all this really good beer
and all this really good red food coloring
and he mixes it all together
and he dumps it all over the fields that Sekhmet has
    scheduled for murdering the next day
so that when she shows up
she just sees a big lake of what she can only assume is
    blood
blood that smells like booze
so, like
the blood of really drunk people?
and she's like "ALL RIGHT
LOOKS LIKE MURDERING IS DONE EARLY
    TODAY
TIME FOR MY SECOND FAVORITE PASTIME:
DEVOURING THE BLOOD OF THE
    INNOCENT."
So Sekhmet just dives right in and starts slurping the
    boozeblood
which is such good shit
that everybody calls it "THE SLEEPMAKER"
and because of that she ends up passing out pretty quick
and she wakes up all hung over

and Ra is like "HaHAAAA
from now on you will be known as Hathor
and the only thing you will kill people with
is KINDNESS."
And basically whatever Ra says just immediately
    happens
so that's who Sekhmet becomes from then on.

So obviously the moral of the story
is that the best way to deal with a rampaging
    psychopath
is to get them really, really drunk.

◆ ◆ ◆

ISIS HAS BAD TASTE
IN JEWELRY

So time passes, and now Osiris is the king of the gods
he thinks he's hot shit, with his godly appendages up
    whole vast swathes of blouse.
But meanwhile there's this dick Set.
That is his name
Set.
I'm not talking about some kind of dick set
such as you might purchase for an adult tea party.
I am talking about the Egyptian god of the desert
and also storms, darkness, and chaos.
Basically if you are not having a good time
Set is right there, flipping you off with both hands
while jacking off

with his third hand?
Or maybe with a hand he stole
FROM A BABY.
What I mean is, Set's a dick.

The reason I mention Set
is that he gets all butthurt over not being king of
    the gods
so he has this great plan
which is he makes this coffin out of wood
which is like tailor-made for Osiris basically
and then he calls up all the gods like "HEY, GUYS
YOU SHOULD COME OVER
I'M HAVING A WEIRD COFFIN PARTY."
And all the gods are like "Oh shit, weird coffin party.
We'll be right over."
So they all get there and Set is like "All right
I made this coffin.
Whoever fits perfectly inside it gets candy."
And of course, all the gods think this sounds like an
    awesome idea
so they all take turns trying to get into the coffin
and they all fail
but then it's Osiris's turn
and Osiris is like "I dunno, guys
this seems like a transparent ruse."
but then he gets in the coffin anyway
and it slams shut and locks
and Set lines it with lead and throws it in the Nile river
and everyone is like "Whoa, major coffin-party foul."
and Set is like "So I get to be king now, right?"
AND HE DOES.

So naturally Osiris's wife Isis decides to go find him
so she can at least bury him properly now that he has
    drowned

and she finds out that the coffin has floated all the way
    to Byblos
(which is actually just Lebanon in disguise)
and gotten absorbed by an oak tree
which got cut down
and used to build a support pillar
in a palace
for the king of Byblos.
Shiiiit.

So Isis shows up in Byblos like "Hey queen
my husband is embedded in your palace
may I please extract him?"
And the queen is like "Sure, go ahead.
It's not like he's a major structural support or anything,
    right?"
and Isis is like "Haha, sucker."
And she goes and removes the pillar
WITHOUT DAMAGING THE PALACE AT ALL
thus inventing Jenga.

Except instead of delicately placing the coffin on top of
    the palace
Isis takes out Osiris's body and drags it back to Egypt
and buries it in the desert
so he can finally rest in peace
apparently forgetting
that Set is the GOD OF THE DESERT.
So Set very quickly sniffs out Osiris's grave
and is like "Hmm
I haven't fucked with this guy enough.
How about I tear him into fourteen pieces
and then EAT HIS DICK."
So that is what he does
and he chucks the other thirteen pieces all the fuck
    everywhere

and then Isis is like "What is that noise?
It better not be my husband getting ripped up and
    thrown everywhere."
BUT IT IS TOO LATE
IT HAS ALREADY HAPPENED
and Isis finds out and she is like "Seriously?
I just buried this guy.
Now I gotta go find all these body parts
and bury them AGAIN
even though Set will prolly just find them again
and rip them into SMALLER pieces."
Anyway, she manages to find all the pieces
(which have turned into full moons by the way)
except for his dick
because like I said
SET ATE IT
so Isis is like "Maaaan
Osiris's dick was like
the most important part of his personality"
so what she does
is she makes a GOLD COCK
and she hangs it around her neck
and BAM
Osiris is alive again
with a golden dong
thus laying the groundwork for Mike Myers's
    cinematic triumph, *Goldmember*
and also getting Isis pregnant with Horus
because I guess that dick necklace was more potent
    than she bargained for.

So ladies
I guess the moral of the story is
don't wear a cock around your neck
because unplanned pregnancy
is the WORST accessory.

◆ ◆ ◆

THOTH IS JUST GIVING
OUT SCORPIONS

So Osiris is back in action
and his dick is more blinged out than ever
BUT ALL IS NOT WELL
because as soon as Osiris gets resurrected
ISIS GIVES BIRTH TO THIS DUDE NAMED
    HORUS.
Actually, that is not the bad part
because Horus is a pretty cool dude, honestly.
No, see, the bad part
is that seeing as Set was totally willing to EAT
    OSIRIS'S DICK
just to prevent him from getting a proper burial
all signs point toward he is going to murder the CRAP
    out of this baby
especially since Horus is totally fated to murder Set if
    he ever gets old enough.

So Isis is pretty careful about keeping her baby away
    from murder
but then one day, Set is like "HEY, ISIS
COME INTO THIS SPINNING MILL."
and Isis is like "SPINNING MILL, HOORAY."
And then Set is like "Oh, did I say spinning mill?
I meant WRETCHED IMPRISONMENT
FOREVER
I AM SORRY FOR THE CONFUSION
JUST KIDDING, TOTALLY NOT SORRY."

So Isis is understandably upset about this
and so is this super-wise dude named Thoth
so he comes down and is like "Hey, Isis
how would you like to escape this prison?"
And Isis is like "I would like that a lot."
so Thoth is like "Boom. You got it.
Here, have some scorpions."
And Isis is like "WHAT, WHY WOULD YOU GIVE
    ME SCORPIONS?"
And Thoth is like "Chill out.
These scorpions will guide you to safety.
I'm the god of wisdom, okay? I've got this handled."
so Isis takes Horus, and they follow these seven
    scorpions for like a WEEK.
No one has any ideas where they are going
probably because the guides in this scenario
are SCORPIONS.
SCORPIONS ARE NOT THE ULTIMATE
    GUIDES, MY FRIENDS.
THEY ARE FANTASTIC AT STINGING THE
    CRAP OUT YOU
BUT I FEEL LIKE THEY ARE NOT KNOWN FOR
    THEIR SENSE OF DIRECTION.

But after a lot of bullshit, Isis and the scorpions and
    Horus finally arrive in some town
and Isis goes and knocks on the door of some rich
    chick's house
and the rich chick is like "Oh, why hello there HOLY
    SHIT SCORPIONS.
NO NO NO NO NO."
But so no sooner has the rich chick slammed her door
than this poor chick is like "Hey there.
I see you have some scorpions.
I'm so poor that I have even pawned my fear of death.
Come crash at my hovel."

But then PLOT TWIST
the scorpions all throw a fit
about not being invited into the other house
so they go inside
and sting the crap out of the rich chick's baby
and she hears the baby crying
and she is like "What's that noise?
I hope it's not the sound of my baby getting stung by
    SCORPIONS.
OH SHIT SCORPIONS."
And Isis hears all this commotion
and she is like "SCORPIONS
    YOU ARE THE SHITTIEST GUIDES.
NOW I HAVE TO SOLVE ALL THE PROBLEMS."
So she runs up to where the baby is busy dying
and she is like "Hey, poison, get out of that baby."
And the poison is like "Maaaan . . . fine."
and then Isis leaves, like "ANOTHER DAY SAVED
THANKS TO ME AND NO THANKS TO THESE
    SCORPIONS."

And then she ends up in the marsh she was supposed
    to check out
and she hides Horus in the mud, like "Okay, son
I am going to bury you in marsh filth now
among poisonous animals
some of which I KNOW to be irritable scorpions
so just try not to move around too much.
I'm gonna go get burgers."
So Isis comes back later
and she is like "Hey, Horus
would you like some burgers?
Hmm . . . you don't seem to be moving at all
or breathing or anything.
Oh noooo.
Set, did you turn into a snake and poison my baby?"

And Set is like "Yup."
And Isis proceeds to scream the most heavy metal
    scream possible
it is so metal that it STOPS THE SUN
or more accurately, THE SUNBOAT.
And Ra is chilling in the boat with all of his hookers
    and stuff
and it stops all of a sudden
with one of those record scratch noises you hear in bad
    teen movies
and everyone is like "Whaaaat?
Thoth, go find out what Isis is angry about."
so Thoth goes down there like "Woman, I hooked you
    up with scorpions and everything. What now?"
and Isis is like "Look, I know you are itching to get
    your bone on in the backseat of the sunboat
but could you do me a solid
and just revive my son real quick?"
and Thoth is like "Oh yeah, no problem. Done.
By the way, how were those scorpions?
Pretty sweet, right?"
and Isis is like "They were a pack of angry scorpions
that you gave to a single mother with a child."

Anyway Horus is alive now
but he and Isis still have to hide out in the marshes
while his balls gather sufficient mass
to allow him to murder Set.

So basically the moral of the story
is that scorpions are only good for one thing
and that one thing is rad tattoos.

◆ ◆ ◆

Horus Jerks Off
in Set's Salad

So Horus grows up
and Isis is like "Hey, son, remember that asshole Set?
The one who you are destined to ruin?"
and Horus is like "I mean
you never stop talking about him
and also he turned into a snake
and poisoned me to death when I was a baby.
That tends to make people pretty memorable
when they do stuff like that."
and Isis is like "Well, why haven't you killed him
    yet?"
and Horus is like "JEEZ, MOM, FINE
GET OFF MY BACK.
HEY, SET, I'M 'BOUT TO KILL YOU
GET READY."
So Set shows up like "OH NO, YOU DIDN'T."
And Horus is like "HOLD STILL FOR A SECOND.
LET ME STAB YOUR FACE."
And Isis is like "OH SHIT, STOP.
I JUST REMEMBERED THAT SET IS MY
    BROTHER."
and Horus tries to break her legs
but then she stabs him
and Set gets away
and Horus is like "Wow, Mom.
Seriously?"
But Isis heals him later so it's fine.

Wait, what am I talking about
shit is so un-fine you could coat sandpaper with it
and then use it to shave off a goat's face.
Because now Set is thinking as HARD AS HE CAN
     about how to screw over Horus
and finally he's like "I KNOW
I will use my SEMEN to solve this problem.
HEY, HORUS, WANNA HAVE SEX?
And Horus is like "Well, normally I would say no
but today I am an idiot, so okay."
and they have a bunch of sweaty sex
but then right at the crucial moment
Horus uses his lightning reflexes to parry Set's
     manbatter
because apparently it's not gay if the jizz stays outside
     your butt.
So then he's got a handful of manana cream pie
and he's like "Eww, what am I going to do with this?
I KNOW, I'LL THROW IT IN A RIVER."
and thus invents hand washing and pollution
SIMULTANEOUSLY
so now HORUS is thinking about how to fuck
     over SET
and he's like "Hmm . . .
Apparently the name of the game
is 'get your semen inside of the other guy's body.'
I don't make the rules
I just make the jizz.
Let's make this happen."
So he sneaks into Set's house and jerks off in his salad
and then Set eats the salad and Horus is like "HAHA
YOU JUST ATE MY SPOOGE."
Is it just me, or is spooge the single least attractive
     synonym for dickglue?
Anyway, Set is like "BULLSHIT.
LET'S GO BEFORE THE REST OF THE GODS

AND NEEDLESSLY AIR OUR DIRTY LAUNDRY
IN HOPES OF DETERMINING SUPERIORITY."
So they call together the other gods
and Set is like "Guys
I totally jizzed in Horus's butt.
That means I'm better than him, right?
and Horus is like "You didn't jizz in my butt.
What are you talking about?
Go ahead and call for your sperm.
See where they're at."
Yeah, apparently these dudes keep in touch with all
    their sperm.
Talk about being a devoted father.
Anyway, Set is like "FINE.
OHHH SPERRMMMM. WHERE AAARE
    YOUUUU?"
And the sperm is like "HERE WE ARE
IN THE RIVER."
and Set is like "Dammit, Horus
Did you block my cock?"
and Horus is like "That is in fact exactly what I did.
Now hold on
lemme find out where my sperm is at real quick."
And the sperm is like "HERE WE ARE
IN SET'S STOMACH."
And Set is like "NOOOO."
And everyone else is like "Wow.
This is astonishingly stupid
how about we settle this pissing contest
with a *reasonable* competition
like a boat race
except the boats are made of stone.
THAT'S PERFECT
THAT'S NOT STUPID AT ALL."
So Set and Horus get their boats ready
but Horus has a secret

which is that his boat is actually MADE OF WOOD
it's just painted to look like stone
which raises a couple of questions:
First of all
why didn't anyone check to see if Horus's boat was
    actually made of stone?
And second of all
since they didn't
WHY DID SET NOT DO THIS?
DOES HE NOT REALIZE THAT STONE IS THE
    WORST THING TO MAKE BOATS OUT OF?
I mean, maybe he thinks they are trying to race to the
    bottom of the lake
in which case I understand
either that or he's SCRUPULOUSLY HONEST
but we're talking about the god of storms, chaos,
    and evil
who has been known to do things like eat the balls of
    his enemies
and then try to kill their babies
and then when their babies grow up
try to have buttsex with the very same babies
so I feel like honesty is not top of his priority list.
But anyway they have the race and Set's boat sinks
and Horus wins
and as a result he gets to be king of Egypt
and Set has to be his bitch forever.

So the moral of the story
is next time you are jockeying for a sweet promotion
consider jizzing in your coworkers' food
but make sure to also brush up on your boat-racing
just in case.

MAYAN

I've never been freaked out by a calendar even a little
just getting a rise out of me with a calendar is a feat on
    its own
but the Mayans are the MVPs of making calendars, man.
You have to hand it to a culture
that can make a calendar SO INTENSE
that it is still freaking people out
CENTURIES LATER.
And they didn't stop at just freaking people out.
No, see, these dudes wrote a whole fan fiction for their
    calendar.
It's called the Popol Vuh
and it is basically just a super-complicated code version
of the calendar itself
secretly translated by some Mayan dudes
around the time that the Spanish were killing
    everybody
and now
it is time to take that sacred and clandestine work
of those brave souls
and mock the shit out of it.

THE MAYANS HAVE THE MOST BRUTAL CALENDAR

So there is this one Mayan dude, right?
he has like fifty goddamn names
Like Hurucan, and Gugumatz, and Heart-of-Sky
and I'm not even really sure if he is one Mayan dude
or like, a collection of Mayan dudes
because they keep acting like he is two people
but the two people never do anything independently
so they're basically just one person
or some kind of hive mind.
Anyway, we're going to call this thing Quetzalcoatl.

Quetzalcoatl is bored, because all there is anywhere
is just a whole bunch of water and some sky
and it's not even interesting sky
because there is no light
so Quetzalcoatl is like "Okay, boom."
And there is some light
and then he goes boom again
and there is some land
but this is still pretty lame because what is the point of
    being able to do this kind of shit
if there is no one around to get freaked out by how cool
    it is?
Now, this may sound pretty familiar so far
but here's where it gets crazy:
Quetzalcoatl's master plan for getting worshippers
is to invent JAGUARS.

And then he's like "WHOA, JAGUARS
LOOK, I JUST FUCKING MADE YOU.
PRETTY NEAT, HUH?"
And the jaguars are all "Rarrrr, we are jaguars.
We can't talk or be impressed."
So Quetzalcoatl is like "Aww, fuck you guys.
I'm gonna make some way more awesome creatures
and they are going to worship me
and you are going to be their SLAVES."
So he gets some dirt
and he makes dirt-people
but the dirt-people really suck
because first of all, they are made out of dirt
second of all, they only speak gibberish
and third of all, they dissolve in water
so Quetzalcoatl figures
that even if they COULD worship him
he would get pretty embarrassed
so he kills all of them by dumping water on them
and then he calls these two other dudes
Xmucane and Xpiacoc
who have names that sound like prescription drugs
designed to treat nasal congestion and erectile
    dysfunction respectively
and he's like "Hey, is it a good idea for me to make
    people out of wood?"
And they say "Yeah, go for it."

So he makes people out of wood
like a whole bunch of wooden robots, basically
and they can speak and walk around
and they don't dissolve in water
but they are TREMENDOUS assholes.
One might even say they have a STICK up their asses.
Get it? Get it?

Aw, screw you guys.
Anyway, they totally forget to worship Quetzalcoatl
even a little bit
and he's getting pretty pissed at this point
because he has seriously made EVERYTHING
    THAT EXISTS
and no one is giving him ANY CREDIT
so he kind of freaks out a little
and causes fire to rain from the sky
and burns everything to cinders
and then makes all of the wood-people's cookware
    come alive and kill them
and all the animals move into their houses and eat
    them
even though they are made of wood
and totally not tasty
and meanwhile Quetzalcoatl makes a bunch of
    ACTUALLY delicious people out of tortillas
and those people are supposedly us
and as soon as Quetzalcoatl gets bored
he is going to make us into burritos
and then feed us to jaguars or whatever
and this story was apparently plausible enough
to freak out THE ENTIRE GODDAMN WORLD
ALL THE WAY THROUGH 2012.
But anyway, everyone lives happily ever after
except the wood-people
who get chased into the woods
and turned into monkeys.

So the moral of the story is
never set fire to a monkey
because it is made out of wood
and you will start a forest fire.

◆ ◆ ◆

Hunahpú and Xbalanqué: ULTIMATE BALLERS

So there are these two dudes
Hun Hunapú and Vucub Hunapú.
They are twins, or at least brothers.
Anyway, they piss off the gods of the underworld
with their constant ball playing.
Yes, that is right
they play sports SO HARD
that it upsets MAYAN SATAN.

Anyway, the gods summon them down to the
    underworld
(which is called Xibalbá
because no Mayan story is complete
without about six thousand proper nouns beginning
    with the letter "X")
and the gods are all "Hey, guys
we heard you like ball playing
GET IT?
WE HEARD.
BECAUSE YOU ARE SO LOUD."
And the twins are like "What of it?"
And the gods are like "Well
if you like ball games so much
how about you play ball with us

FOR YOUR LIIIIVES?!?!"
And the twins are like "This sounds like
THE ULTIMATE RUSH."

Now, if this was a Greek myth
the twins would use some kind of mad skill or insane
    trickery to beat the gods.
But this is a Mayan myth.
The dudes get killed before the game even starts
for smoking a cigar the wrong way
and then they get decapitated and buried under the
    ball court
except for Hun's head
which they put that on a calabash tree for some reason.
This turns out to be a bad idea
because some chick named Xquic walks by
and Hun spits in her hand
and he is such a true man that this causes her to get
    pregnant and she gives birth to TWINS.
Fellas
think you're hot shit because your penis is one and a
    half inch longer than the national average?
try impregnating a random chick in her hand
with your saliva
from a tree
on which someone has deposited YOUR SEVERED
    HEAD.
Wait, wait, I went and read it again
it wasn't even his head
it was just his skull.
Skulls don't even MAKE saliva
so . . . I guess when he still had skin and stuff
he just collected a big glob of spit in there
and he HELD IT.
WAITING.

I want that shit on one of those posters that says
    "HANG IN THERE."

So yeah, Xquic gives birth to twins
they are called Hunahpú and Xbalanqué
and these two guys are alive for like five minutes
before they discover their dad's ball-playing gear
and start playing ball SO GODDAMN HARD
that they piss off the underworld AGAIN
and THEY get summoned down there
and the gods are like "Hey
you may have noticed that severed head
    hanging from that tree by your house.
That was the last dude who kept us awake with his ball
    playing.
That was also your dad, FYI.
Why the hell do you guys even like playing ball this
    much?
Okay, look, do you want to play ball for your lives?"
and the twins are like "THE ULTIMATE RUSH."

So they play ball
and see, if this was a Roman myth
or maybe like a Norse myth
these guys would totally have won and avenged their
    father(s)
but like I said, Mayans are assholes
so the gods win again
and they kill the twins and bury them under the ball
    court.

But there is a TWIST
because it turns out the twins are IMMORTAL
    SOMEHOW
so they dig themselves up and sneak away
and they come up with a crafty plan

which is to come directly back to the underworld,
dressed as traveling performers
and the gods are like "SWEEEET"
because it is boring in Xibalbá
without the constant noise of ball playing.
So Hunahpú and Xbalanqué put on a fantastic show
full of amazing feats.
Maybe they even do an astonishing magic trick
where they make their names easier to fucking type.
But anyway, for the finale
one of them cuts off the other's head
and then puts it back on without any problems.
So all the gods are like "AAAAWESOME!
DO ME DO ME DO ME."
And the twins are like "Sure, okay."
And just go and chop off the gods' heads
without any resistance whatsoever
because that is how slick they are
and then they go dig up their dads and resurrect them
and none of them ever forget how lucky they are
to be able to use their DICKS to get women pregnant.

So the moral of the story
is to ball so hard
mothafuckas wanna murder you and bury you under
    the ball court.

◆ ◆ ◆

ZIPACNA AND THE FOUR HUNDRED BOYS

No, this is not the title of a hard-core Mayan gangbang
    porno.
This is an honest-to-goodness myth
from the Popol Vuh
that just HAPPENS to have four hundred boys in it.
Let's do this:

So Zipacna is the son of this guy named Seven Macaw
who is basically a rogue sun god
who hangs out on Earth and causes problems.
Zipacna is responsible for making all the mountains
and he has a bro named Earthquake who is
    responsible for
PUPPIES.
Wait, no, it's earthquakes.
Sorry, I read that wrong.
Look, none of that is really that important
except to establish that Zipacna is the sort of dude
who CAUSES MOUNTAINS.

So Zipacna is taking a bath in the river one day
and these four hundred boys waltz by
carrying a big tree they just chopped down to make
    their house with.
They had to chop down a big tree, you see
because there are four hundred of them.
They are having some trouble, though

because I guess their eyes were bigger than their
    biceps.
They are just dropping this tree all over the place
and Zipacna sees them and he's like "Dudes
let me help you with that."
And then he just picks up the tree all by himself
and takes it to the boys' crib-in-progress
and doesn't even ask for a tip or anything.
Zipacna is a pretty nice dude.
He is the only one.

'Cause see, then what happens
is the four hundred boys have a meeting
and they're all like "Guys
Zipacna just did us a major solid.
How should we reward him for his altruism?
Oh
how about WITH MURDER?
Seriously, we cannot have any really strong dudes
running around being stronger than us.
We have an inferiority complex!
Or rather
we have FOUR HUNDRED INFERIORITY
    COMPLEXES."

So they come up with this brilliant plan
which is that they call up Zipacna and they're like
"Hey, man
thanks for all your help with that big log
but we have another problem now
we need a really big hole for some reason.
We need you to come dig us a really big hole
and then stay in it while we bury you alive.
Okay?"
And Zipacna is like "Anything I can do to help."
But Zipacna is too crafty for their clever ploy!

I mean he digs the hole, sure
but he also digs a special SIDE HOLE to hide in
when the four hundred boys try to bury him.
Actually they don't even try to bury him
they just try to drop a big-ass log down the hole and
    crush him
which is dumb, because he just lifted one of those
    for them
and that is why they wanted to kill him in the first
    place.
But either way, it doesn't matter because Zipacna is
    safe in his side hole.

So the boys are all up on the surface
celebrating their dumb plan
but then they're like "Wait!
If Zipacna was really dead
we would have heard his death cry just now!"
And Zipacna is like "Oh, uh . . .
Owwww, I'm dead now."
And the boys are like "PERFECT.
But WAIT!
If Zipacna is really dead
then a bunch of ants will probably show up the day
    after tomorrow to eat his tasty corpse.
Let's wait for that to happen so we can make sure he's
    really dead."
So Zipacna just chops off all his hair
and bites off all his fingernails
and when the ants show up
he just gives all his hair and fingernails to the ants
and they all scamper all over the place
carrying his body stuff
because I guess ants think hair is delicious?
Reason number a million not to be an ant.
Anyway, then the boys are TOTALLY CONVINCED.

So obviously they all go get trashed
to celebrate their totally bogus victory
and meanwhile Zipacna tunnels out of his hole
and then he crushes all four hundred boys
inside the house he helped them build.

So the moral of the story
is that I don't care what your mom says
biting your fingernails may just save your life.

Judeo-christian

JUDEO-CHRISTIAN

So here's a religion you may have heard of.
In fact, I am willing to bet that nine out of ten of you
when you hear the word "religion"
think of this one first.
But did you know
that this popular high-school jock of religions
is JUST AS SUPREMELY MESSED UP as all the
    other ones?
Yeah, no foolin'.
And it's even crazier
because what masquerades as a single holy book
is actually more like a short-story collection
by like a million crazy desert dudes!
I'm mainly gonna focus on the Old Testament in this
    section
because the Old Testament God gets up to some
    seriously brutal shit
but the New Testament
(the one with Jesus in it and stuff)
is messed up in a whole other way.
OKAY, ENOUGH TALK
LET THE FIASCOS BEGIN!

◆ ◆ ◆

GOD MAKES A LOT
OF STUFF

Okay so God, right?

No, I didn't leave out any letters up there.
That is not a typo.
No, see, in this pantheon
THERE IS ONLY ONE GOD.
I KNOW.
PRETTY LAME.
But anyway, this God guy is facing a problem that you
    should be pretty familiar with at this point.
The problem is that there is water
AND NOTHING ELSE.
ALSO IT'S SUPER DARK.
So BAM, he invents light, day one
and then he misses the dark part
so he invents night too
and then he's like "Oh, looks like it's nighttime.
Better go to sleep."

DAY TWO:
God basically just makes a big divider
right in the middle of the water
and all the water below the line is earth
and all the water above the line is heaven.
(This is why angels are traditionally depicted wearing
    scuba gear.)

Day three is when God finally gets around to inventing
    dry land.
Seriously?
It took Ra like all of thirty seconds
to invent dry land AND HIMSELF.
Is this just not something that occurred to God
until he had two nights to sleep on it?
Oh, and he makes plants too.

On day four God invents the sun and the moon and
    the stars
which begs the question
WHERE WAS THE LIGHT COMING FROM
    BEFORE?
And then he's like "Oh shit, the moon.
Better go to sleep."
This dude needs an awful lot of sleep for an
    omnipotent dude
which may explain why wars happen.

So on day five, God invents animals.
ESPECIALLY WHALES.
The Bible is very specific on this point.

By day six, God is pretty pleased.
He's like "Wow, this is awesome.
How can I ruin it?"
So he invents mankind
and also cows
because he forgot about cows.
Then he gets real hammered to celebrate
and he passes out on Saturday
and doesn't wake up until MONDAY.
In fact he sleeps through Sunday SO HARD
that NO ONE IS ALLOWED TO DO WORK ON
    SUNDAY EVER AGAIN.

That is a true power nap.

So when he finally wakes up
he makes this garden called the Garden of Eden
and he puts the guy he made in there
and the man (whose name is Adam) is like "God, I'm
    bored."
and God is like "Ooh, I know a great game we can play.
It's called name all the animals.
Ready? Go."
So Adam falls for this transparent ruse to get him to do
    God's work for him
and he names all the animals
but then he gets done doing that
and he is like "Still bored, God."
And God is like "Okay, I got this."
And BAM
knocks him out and steals one of his ribs.
This is some straight-up Tijuana shit is what this is.

So Adam wakes up in a bathtub full of ice
like "Whaaaat happened?"
and God is like "Look, dude, I made you a chick.
She is made of your rib, so she might be kinda dumb
I tried just making one out of clay, like how I made you
but she was harboring all these problematic delusions
    of equality
so I had to find a workaround
anyway, she's totally hot, so don't worry about it.
Oh, by the way, I should warn you guys
you can totally eat from any tree in the garden
EXCEPT FOR THE TREE OF KNOWLEDGE OF
    GOOD AND EVIL
THAT ONE OVER THERE
THE TOTALLY UNGUARDED ONE WITH THE
    DELICIOUS-LOOKING APPLES"

and Adam and Eve are like "Okay, whatever dude"
(Eve is the name of the chick God made, by the way)
and they go off somewhere to bone.

But there is a SERPENT in this garden.
I think he is supposed to be Satan
but really I think he's just a serpent
who happens to be a big jerk.
This serpent runs up on Eve when she is off on her own
and he is like "Hey, gurl, try one of these apples."
And Eve is like "YOU MEAN THE APPLES OF
    KNOWLEDGE?
THE ONES THAT GOD EXPLICITLY FORBID
    US FROM EATING??
NOOOO WAY."
And the serpent is like "No, come on."
And Eve is like "Okay."
So she eats the apple
and it is DELICIOUS
and so she takes the rest of it to Adam, all like "Here,
    eat this."
And Adam is like "What? No, God said if we ate that
    then we would die or something."
And Eve is like "Uhhh . . . totally still alive over here."
And Adam is like "Okay, fair point."
So he eats the apple
and suddenly both of them realize
HOW INCREDIBLY NAKED THEY ARE.
THIS IS WHAT THE TREE DOES
IT LETS YOU KNOW YOU'RE NAKED
THE MYTHICAL TREE OF KNOWLEDGE OF
    GOOD AND EVIL
COULD HAVE EASILY BEEN REPLACED
BY A FIVE-DOLLAR MIRROR
FROM A COLOMBIAN BROTHEL.

So they make themselves some clothes, 'cause they're
    embarrassed
and then God wakes up from one of his meganaps
and he's like "HEY
WHO THE FUCK TOLD YOU YOU WERE
    NAKED?"
See, this was his big plan.
His big plan was just to look at naked people all day.
Now the plan is ruined
so he responds in the rational way
which is to put curses on everybody
and then kick them out of his garden.
He curses the serpent to have to crawl on its belly
    forever
apparently forgetting
that that is what SERPENTS DO ALL THE TIME
and he curses Eve to undergo tremendous pain during
    childbirth
because apparently he is able to imagine some crazy
    parallel universe
where pushing something the size of a screaming
    football out of your vag
is somehow NOT INCREDIBLY PAINFUL
and then he curses Adam to toil endlessly
and Adam is like "Come on!
Couldn't you just curse me to like . . .
have testicles or something?"
But by then he is already kicked out of Eden
and there is a big flaming sword guarding the door
and there is nothing left to do
but have a bunch of kids
and try to forget the whole fiasco.

So the moral of the story
is to never be naked

because God is a creepy pervert
who invented you so he could look at your junk.

◆ ◆ ◆

CAIN AND ABEL INVENT
THE SIBLING RIVALRY

So Adam and Eve know each other.
Oh wait
I read that wrong.
Adam and Eve totally have SEX with each other.
It's just that the Bible is cagey about shit like that
so instead of writing "Adam boned Eve
in a moist, raunchy sex fiasco."
the Bible guys would put "Adam KNEW Eve
in a moist, raunchy sex fiasco."
It's awesome once you know about it
and now you do.

BUT SO ANYWAY
Adam and Eve bang the daylights out of each other
and they have two kids: Cain and Abel
and these dudes are farmers
because what else are they gonna do?
No one has built any of the cool stuff yet.
So Abel becomes a sheep farmer
and Cain becomes a vegetables farmer.
Then harvest time comes
(I am guessing that harvest time for sheep
is whenever they start to piss you off)

and Abel makes an offering to the LORD
(always in all caps, by the way)
of like, the fattest sheep he owns.
Dude, he could have totally eaten that.
MEANWHILE
Cain makes an offering
of all his choicest vegetables
and God gets all of these things
and he is like "OH SNAP
DELICIOUS LAMB MEAT
THAT I HAVE NO USE FOR BECAUSE I AM
    IMMORTAL AND OMNIPOTENT AND
    STUFF.
GOOD JOB, ABEL.
BUT WHAT THE FUCK IS THIS SHIT, CAIN?
VEGETABLES?
IF I WANTED TO EAT VEGETABLES
WHY DO YOU THINK I INVENTED MEAT
HUH?
YOU'RE NOT MY DAD, CAIN.
YOU DON'T KNOW WHAT'S BEST FOR ME."

So Cain goes and hits up Abel later.
He's like "Yo, bro
God really dug your offering, huh?"
and Abel is like "Yeah, well, it was pretty sweet."
And Cain is like "Yeah . . . yeah . . .
Hey listen, I actually dug something of yours as well."
And Abel is like "Oh yeah, what is it?"
And Cain is like "YOUR GRAVE,
    MOTHERFUCKER!"
Then he stabs him and puts him underground
thus SINGLE-HANDEDLY INVENTING
    MURDER.
Yeah
before this, murder didn't even exist.

Cain is seriously like the Thomas Edison of stabbing
    people.

So pretty soon God comes poking around
like "HEY, ABEL
ME AND THE HOLY GHOST ARE HAVING A
    BARBECUE.
GOT ANY MORE OF THAT DELICIOUS LAMB
    MEAT?"
And then he sees Cain and he's like "OH HEY,
    DIPSHIT
NO, I DON"T WANT ANY VEGETABLES
THERE IS NOT GOING TO BE A 'VEGAN
    OPTION' AT THIS BARBECUE.
HEY, HAVE YOU SEEN YOUR BROTHER
    ANYWHERE?"
And Cain is like "What? Noooo.
What am I, my brother's babysitter or some shit?
Find him yourself."
And God is like "Oh hold on, I'm getting a phone call.
Hello?
Oh hi, Abel's blood.
What's that?
Cain murdered you and hid you underground
foolishly believing that six feet of dirt would obscure
    you from THE OMNISCIENT CREATOR?!
YOU DON'T SAY.
CAIN, YOU ARE SO GETTING PUNISHED."

So he curses Cain
so that the earth will refuse to get farmed by him
and he has to roam forever and everyone will hate him
and Cain is like "But, Godddd
now everyone I meet is just gonna kill me."
And God is like "Oh, good point.
How about I make a law that says no one can kill you

and I put a mark on you to let everyone know
that you are a dude not to kill?"
And Cain is like "Uh . . . *yes.*"
At this stage of the Bible, God is not very good at
    coming up with punishments.
Don't worry, he gets way better.
But yeah, then Cain goes off to live in the land of Nod
and everyone is either unhappy or dead or omnipotent.

So the moral of the story
is that God hates vegetarians.

◆ ◆ ◆

Abraham Is Totally Cool About Stabbing His Kid in the Face

Seriously?
SERIOUSLY?
Okay, here we go:

So one day this guy named Abraham is out working in
    the fields
and God is like "Abraham! Abraham! Hey!"
Abraham is like "Chill out, I'm right here.
What do you want?"
And God is like "You know your son?"
And Abraham is like "My only son?
Yeah, you could say I know him."
And God is like "Okay, here's what I want you to do:

I want you to take your son
up to a mountain that I'm gonna show you
and I want you to kill him and set him on fire for me."
And Abraham is like "Okay, well
I guess you know what you're doing."

So Abraham goes and gets his son
and he's like "Come on, son, let's go on a nice father-
    son trip to a mountain that God will show us.
We are going to make a blood sacrifice
it will be a great bonding experience."
So they start going to the mountain
along with some donkeys, and some slaves
which God is apparently cool with
and Abraham makes his son carry the wood
and he carries the fire and the knife
and halfway there, his son is like
"Uhh, Dad?"
And Abraham is like "What?"
And his son is like "Dad
where is the lamb we're gonna sacrifice?"
And Abraham is like "Uh . . . well . . .
God is going to provide a lamb for us, son."
HE IS REMARKABLY CALM ABOUT THIS
    WHOLE THING.
PERHAPS FOR ABRAHAM
ONE SON IS TOO MANY SONS.

So anyway, they get to the mountain
and Abraham straps his son down
and his son doesn't say anything
presumably because the level of shitty parenting going
    on here has rendered him speechless
and Abraham raises up the knife
and God is like "WHOA, WHOA, ABRAHAM!!!!"
and Abraham is like "WHAT?!

I'm kind of in the middle of something right now."
And God is like "Haha, PSYCH!
I was totally just kidding about the whole sacrificing
    your son thing.
But, dude, that was HARD-CORE.
Tell you what, man
I like a man with big balls
so how about I make it so that your children WILL
    OUTNUMBER THE STARS IN THE SKY."
And Abraham is like "WHAT
THAT IS TOO MANY KIDS."
and God is like "Haha, no need to thank me, buddy.
Your thoughtless attempted sacrifice of your own son
    is all the thanks I need."
And then Abraham finds a ram
which he sacrifices to God instead of his son
and then I guess the two of them go home
or actually, they go to a place called Beersheba
which is clearly the party city of ancient times
and I like to imagine that they partied so hard
that afterward they had to go to Bathsheba
just to wash the stank off
and things are pretty awkward between Abraham and
    his son from then on
but it's okay, because Abraham has a ton more kids.

So the moral of the story
is that it's never a bad idea
to try to set your kids on fire
as long as the voices tell you so.

✦ ✦ ✦

NOAH IS ON A BOAT

So God makes a bunch of people
they fuck up and kill each other
but then they feel bad about it
so they have, like, CRAZY makeup sex
and the next NINE THOUSAND PAGES OF THE
    BIBLE
(depending on how big you make the text)
are about all the babies people made
because the Bible predates condoms
and I think we should all remember this.

So everyone has a bunch of kids
but it doesn't matter
because apparently they all suck
and God decides he's had enough of this shit.
He's just gonna kill everybody
kinda like that other god in that Mayan myth.
See what I mean about how all this junk starts to run
    together after a while?
And he totally rips off Quetzalcoatl even harder
because his method of choice for killing everyone
is a GIANT FLOOD
(P.S.:
Did you know that whenever H. P. Lovecraft uses the
    word "antediluvian"
what he means is "predating the biblical flood?"
Because yeah

apparently H. P. Lovecraft knows EXACTLY WHEN
    THIS HAPPENED.)

But God can't just kill EVERYONE
because he put a lot of work into this whole humanity
    thing
so he picks the least sucky dude in the world
whose name is Noah
and he's like "YO, NOAH!
EVERYBODY'S GOING TO DIE, EXCEPT YOU
CONGRATULATIONS.
HOPE YOU DON'T HAVE ANY FRIENDS.
GONNA NEED YOU TO BUILD A REAL BIG
    BOAT, BUDDY
BUT NO FRIENDS ALLOWED ON THIS
    BOAT
JUST ANIMALS
SEVEN PAIRS OF EVERY KID OF ANIMAL
(unless they are really filthy
in which case you can just get one pair)
'CAUSE YEAH, I SPENT A LOT OF TIME ON
    THOSE ANIMALS
BUT I FORGOT TO MAKE THEM SMART
    ENOUGH TO BUILD BOATS
SO THAT IS YOUR JOB NOW."

So this sounds like a lot of work to Noah
but hey, it's better than dying
so he gets some lumber and he gets to work
and somehow he manages to pull it off in time
with all his neighbors showing up at his house and
    calling him an idiot all day.
Well, joke's on them.
They all die.
But then, joke's on Noah

because now he has to live on a boat
full of nothing but animals and his wife.
Nobody wins except for God
who is playing a game called "Do Whatever the Hell I
Want Because I'm God"

So anyway, the whole world stays flooded
for FORTY DAYS
which is actually just Bible speak
for AN ARBITRARILY LONG TIME
but Noah is patient
because, oh yeah, I forgot to tell you:
NOAH IS SIX HUNDRED YEARS OLD.
Okay, now I'm super impressed.
This six-hundred-year-old dude managed to build a
massive boat in just a couple months
AND
MORE IMPRESSIVELY
he managed to live six hundred years on Earth
without committing ANY MORTAL SINS.

So anyway, the rain stops eventually
and Noah's family and all the animals
are getting pretty antsy
no pun intended
because only some of them are actually ants
but anyway, Noah's solution is to send birds out to find
land.
First he tries sending out a raven
but that's useless.
The raven pretty much just flies back and forth a lot.
So Noah sends out a dove
and the dove fails to find land
so Noah KEEPS sending it out
until on the third try
it finally brings back an olive branch

indicating that it found a tree somewhere
and this somehow became an international symbol for
    peace
when what it SHOULD symbolize is "HOORAY
WE ARE NO LONGER COVERED IN WATER."

So yeah, after that everything is pretty straightforward.
They find some land
and Noah makes an altar
and God makes a rainbow
which is his way of saying "Sorry, dudes
won't happen again."
And he has kept that promise
SO FAR.

So the moral of the story
is that if you are planning on being a terrible person
    your whole life
you can just keep a big boat in your garage
and you'll be totally safe.

❖ ❖ ❖

KING SOLOMON AND THE
DISPOSABLE BABY

So there's this king named Solomon.
It doesn't really matter what he's king of.
You know how it was in Bible times.
Kings all over the place.
But the thing about Solomon

is that unlike most of the kings who were all over the
    place in Bible times
Solomon is INCREDIBLY WISE.
Observe:

So one of the things a king used to have to do
was to sit in a room
while people shouted their problems at him
and then solve the problems using his king powers.
So one day, Solomon is doing this
and two ladies walk in with a dead baby, a live baby
and a SERIOUS DOOZY OF A PROBLEM.
One woman is like "Hey, Solomon
I gave birth to this healthy baby five days ago
but then my bitch of a roommate
gave birth to a DEAD baby two days later
and she thought it would be a good idea
to pull some Indiana Jones shit
and switch my live baby for her dead one.
Make her give me my baby back."
And the other woman is like "Nuh-uh!
This is totally my baby
your baby DIED because you are a terrible parent."

So Solomon is like "Hmm, this is a tough one.
Oh wait, no, it's not. I have swords.
Hey, guards
cut the baby in half
give a piece to each of these ladies.
PROBLEM SOLVED."
And the first lady is like "Jesus Christ
just give her the baby.
What is wrong with you?"
And the second woman is like
"DIBS ON THE TOP HALF."
And Solomon is like "Ah-HAH!

The baby must belong to the first lady
because mothering instincts generally prevent people
from agreeing to bisect their babies
and even if the first lady ISN'T the mother
the baby should still probably go to the woman who is
    NOT WILLING TO CUT IT WITH SWORDS.
Seriously, lady
what were you even planning on doing with the top
    half of a baby?
You've already got 100 percent of a dead baby
no questions asked.
What are you, making a casserole?
Case dismissed."

So the moral of the story
is you should always do a background check
on all your potential roommates.

HINDU

No culture before or since
has so flawlessly combined the disparate realms
of brutal murder
and epic dance battles
as did the ancient Hindus
which I suppose makes sense
coming from the nation that gave us Bollywood.
People in Hindu myths are ready to cut a rug at the
    drop of a hat
and they are also ready to cut other things
and in fact, maybe the reason that the hat dropped in
    the first place
was that someone cut off the head it was resting on
and then ate it
because that's how the Hindu gods roll
but it is not all decapitation and bump 'n' grind, my
    friends
Hindu mythology gets up to some seriously cosmic
    shit as well.
Observe:

◆ ◆ ◆

THE HINDUS LIKE
TO CHOP DUDES UP

So back in the days before there was stuff and things
there was a dude.
Just this one dude, as far as the eye could see
spanning the entire breadth of the universe, plus like
ten extra feet for good measure.
His name
was the Dude
but not the Dude from *The Big Lebowski*.
This is a significantly Bigger Lebowski we are talking
    about here.
This is a Lebowski as Big as the entirety of creation.
He is so big that he exists at all times
both before and after his birth
and like a quarter of his body is made up of all the
    animals ever
and the other three-fourths is all the gods
and he actually gives birth to a dude named Virj
who then gives birth to HIM.
WHAT.

So obviously the gods get tired of trying to
    conceptualize this universal dude
and they're like "Screw this, let's sacrifice him."
So they tie him down and cut him up
and just start flinging pieces of his body
ABSOLUTELY EVERYWHERE
and all the giblets start turning into things

like all the tasty clarified butter they boil off him turns
        into ANIMALS
even though I thought animals were already a quarter
        of his body.
I guess a quarter of his body was butter?
Fatty.
Anyway, the gods are pretty much making up
        ceremonies as they go along
so those kind of get written down and preserved for all
        eternity.
Also, I gotta hand it to these gods
it takes some serious effort/*cojones*
to kill and butcher someting
that is 75 percent COMPOSED OF YOU.
But anyway, his mouths become priests
and his arms become nobles
and his thighs become the general rabble
and his feet become the slaves.
His brain turns into the moon and his eyeballs are
        the sun
and the sky comes out of his ears and the ground forms
        under his peasant feet
and the gods make sure to start a whole assload of fires
because if you're gonna butcher the universe
it might as well also be on fire
and those fires turn into the IDEAL SOCIAL ORDER
        somehow.
No one mentions what happens to the Dude's dong
or his chest actually.
My guess is that some creeper god stole that shit
        and built himself a pan-galactic RealDoll.

So the moral of the story
is next time you are getting sexed up
just remember that both you and your honey
are made out of the same dude

so basically
everybody is gay.

❖ ❖ ❖

SHIVA CANNOT BE STOPPED

Okay, so there is this dude Brahma, right?
He is the creator of everything.
So one day
he takes his mind
and makes a hot chick come out of it.
This hot chick is his daughter.
But as soon as he pops out this brainbaby
Brahma is like "OH DAMN.
I WANT TO DO THINGS TO THAT
THAT HAVEN'T EVEN BEEN INVENTED YET.
GOOD THING I AM THE CREATOR
AND CAN INVENT THOSE THINGS RIGHT
     AWAY."
And then he goes ahead and gives himself THREE
     EXTRA HEADS
so he can check out his daughter from all angles
thus causing the world to get divided
into four directions
because the creator suddenly desires something that is
     outside himself.
BUT ENOUGH SPIRITUALITY.
BACK TO TITS AND BAD DECISIONS.

Okay, so Brahma's daughter gets wind
of all this exquisite voyeurism going down

and she gets pretty embarrassed
and since she can't stop being hot
she decides to stop being on Earth instead
and she goes up to heaven.
So now Brahma is like "AUGH.
I WANT TO CONTINUE TO LOOK AT TITS
BUT MY HEADS ONLY LOOK DOWN.
LOOKS LIKE I NEED ANOTHER HEAD."
See this is the thing about being the creator.
You do not consider options such as
oh, I don't know
moving your neck.
NO.
You grow an extra fucking head
looking STRAIGHT UP
and then you send it shooting toward heaven
all like "NOM NOM NOM, TITS TIME."

So at this point
Brahma's daughter is up in heaven
like "What am I going to do about this encroaching
     molester head?"
and this is when Shiva steps up to the plate
like "THAT IS ENOUGH BULLSHIT, BRAHMA."
Then he chops off Brahma's head
USING ONLY HIS THUMBNAIL.

But instead of a hearty thank-you
and maybe some victory poontang
Shiva gets Brahma's gross skull stuck to his hand
and he is like "AW BALLS.
THIS IS MY JERKIN'-IT HAND"
And he transforms into Bhairava
aka THE SHIVA OF ULTIMATE RAGE
and he is like "HERE IS WHAT I AM GOING
     TO DO:

I AM GOING TO WRECK SOME SHIT
AND THEN I AM GOING TO *WRECK
SOME SHIT*."
And Brahma is like "Oh no you are not, son.
You are going to get banished all the way on out of here
that is what you are going to do
and then you are going to roam around the land
as a mad beggar
until you get arbitrarily forgiven."
So this is exactly what Shiva does
until one day he stumbles upon a group of sages
all sitting around praying the bajeezus out of
    themselves
and Shiva rolls up
like "HEY HEY, OOGA-BOOGA
CRAZY HOMELESS GUY HERE, WHAT'S UP?"
And the sages are like "What."
And the sages' wives are like "OH MAN, I WANNA
    TAP THAT LIKE A KEG O' BONERS."
and they all go dance the crazy wango-bango tango
    with Shiva
and the sages are like "WHAT."

So obviously they send a tiger after Shiva
and Shiva responds
by TAKING OFF THE TIGER'S SKIN
and WEARING IT AS A SKIRT.
So then they send a poisonous snake after Shiva
and Shiva picks up the snake
and WEARS IT AS A GODDAMN NECKLACE.
So then they send an evil dwarf after Shiva
rightly assuming that there is probably no way for
    Shiva to wear a dwarf.
(That's right, guys.
They have fuckable gold in India too.)
But Shiva just sort of kicks the dwarf over

stands on his face
and takes his club.
Then he turns around like "COME ON, HOT
    BITCHES.
FOLLOW ME INTO THE FOREST."
So they do
and then Shiva (aka Bhairava, remember)
goes to Vishnu's crib
like "Hey, Vishnu, lemme in"
and Vishnu's bouncer is like "Who are you?
You're not on the list."
And Bhairava is like "I AM THE GUY WHO IS
    STABBING YOU TO DEATH WITH A
    TRIDENT."
And then Vishnu jumps out of the back room
like "OH SNAP
I WILL SHOOT BLOOD OUT OF MY FACE AT
    YOU UNTIL YOU GO AWAY."
And Bhairava fills Brahma's sticky skull with Vishnu's
    blood
like "THANKS, SUCKER.
I WAS JUST DROPPING BY TO ASK IF I COULD
    BORROW A CUP OF YOUR BLOOD."
And then he dances off into the forest
carrying the doorkeeper's body
and a skull full of blood.
He dances all over everywhere
until he gets to the holy city Varanasi
at which point he is pardoned for his crimes
and gets to go back to heaven
. . . ?

So I guess the moral of the story
is if you are ever indicted for murder
your best bet
is to do more murders

and then fill the skulls of your victims
with the blood from your other victims
and maybe stage an impromptu dance party
with some women you stole
and eventually people will realize
that you can't be stopped
and you can go to heaven.
Excuse me while I go convert to Hinduism.

❖ ❖ ❖

ANYTHING KALI CAN DO, SHIVA CAN DO BETTER

So we've established that Shiva's a badass
but it turns out that his main job
is to make sure his wife Kali
who is the goddess of having a thousand furious arms
covered in knives and murder
doesn't get too shitfaced off all the blood she drinks
and destroy the world
like this one time
where he lies in front of her on the battlefield
or this other time
when he turns into a baby
like "WAH WAH, TITS PLEASE"
and Kali is overcome
by MOTHERING INSTINCTS.
But there is one particular instance of Shiva handling
    Kali's shit
that is particularly fantastic:

Okay, so this story begins like all stories about Kali:
Kali just killed a bunch of dudes.
Probably they were demons
but really, who knows?
Anyway, to celebrate
Kali takes up residence in a nearby forest
with a bunch of her asshole friends
and starts terrorizing the countryside
stabbing the villagers
then stabbing their stab wounds
then stabbing the blood in their stab wounds
on and on, till the break of dawn
and then after the break of dawn too.

So finally one of the villagers
who is sick of getting stabbed every day
and is also a follower of Shiva
comes running up to Shiva like "HEY, SHIVA
CAN YOU HANDLE THIS SHIT FOR US?
WE REALLY NEED THIS SHIT HANDLED."
and Shiva is like "Dude, can't you see I am busy
ripping tigers in half or something?"
And the dude is like "KALI IS STABBING
        EVERYONE.
SHE MIGHT DESTROY THE WORLD EVEN,
        WHO KNOWS?"
And Shiva is like "Okay, my schedule just cleared up."
So Shiva shows up in the forest
and Kali is like "HEY, DICKFACE."
And Shiva is like "Hey, Kali.
We've talked about this.
You need to stop stabbing all the time.
This right here?
This is what is known as *too much stabbing*."
And Kali is like "NEVER STOP STABBING."

And Shiva is like "That is in fact the opposite of what I
	said.
All right, this is going nowhere.
How about this:
We have a dance contest
and when I utterly hand you your shit in the contest
you agree to stop stabbing for a while?"
And Kali is like "OH BITCH
YOU ARE ABOUT TO GET SERVED."
So they drag out the boom box
spread out the cardboard
dust off their dopest moves
AND PROCEED TO BUST THOSE
	MOTHERFUCKERS LIKE TEAR-AWAY
	PANTS.
These moves they are busting?
Guys:
They are ludicrous moves.
Like, remember the dance contest in *Pulp Fiction*?
This was nothing like that.
John Travolta is terrible at doing the twist.
This is way better.

But finally, Shiva busts out the ULTIMATE MOVE:
THE TANDAVA DANCE
which is just basically a super-energetic dance
and I guess Kali is so tired from stabbing
that she cannot match his dance moves
and so she reluctantly agrees to stop murdering for a
	couple days and go home.
AND THUS BOLLYWOOD WAS BORN.

So the moral of the story
is that we could end all wars forever
if we just weaponized THE POWER OF DANCE.

❖ ❖ ❖

GANESH IS THE VERY DEFINITION OF AN UNPLANNED PREGNANCY

So Shiva is married to Kali, right?

WRONG.
Well yes, Shiva is married to Kali
but as it turns out
Shiva is ALSO married to this other chick Parvati
who is a gentle goddess of life and stuff.
BUT
as it turns out
Parvati and Kali
ARE THE SAME PERSON
WHOA, SNAP, PLOT TWIST.
Yeah, apparently she can transform
between sweet loving life goddess
and unspeakable hurricane of death
for ANY REASON
at ANY TIME.
This is what is known as an exciting marriage.

Anyway, in this story Parvati is busy being Parvati
which is good news for everybody
except for Shiva
because now all the time Kali would have spent
murdering and busting sweet dance moves
Parvati spends thinking about having babies

and Shiva is not ready to be a father.
I mean
he kind of created the entire universe
but he does NOT want to be tied down, okay?
So Parvati gets sick of bugging him to have a baby
    with her
and she's like "Wait a second . . .
I'm a goddess . . .
Having babies in unconventional ways is what
    we DO."
So she just goes ahead and makes a baby all by herself
and she names him Ganesh
and then goes to take a shower
and tells Ganesh to guard the door
because apparently her sole motivation
behind having kids
is to make sure no one sees any naked boobs while she
    is washing up.
IT WOULD HAVE PROBABLY BEEN SIMPLER
    TO JUST LOCK THE DOOR, PARVATI.
CHILDREN ARE A SERIOUS RESPONSIBILITY.

And of course this is the exact moment that Shiva
    decides to come along
and prove beyond a shadow of a doubt
that neither of these people should have kids
because he sees the shower house
where his wife is showering
and he's like "Oh man
what a perfect opportunity for steamy shower sex!"
So he just marches on over there
except instead of getting inside
he gets some impudent baby blocking his path
and Shiva is like "DO YOU KNOW WHO I AM?"
And Ganesh is like "No, dude. I'm a baby."
And Shiva is like "WELL THEN

YOU CAN CALL ME
THE GUY WHO JUST CHOPPED OFF YOUR
     HEAD JUST NOW.
ZING."
And OF COURSE
this is the moment that Parvati chooses to finish her
     shower
and she comes sauntering out of the shower house
and sees her husband standing over her dead baby
and she's like "SHIVAAAA
YOU BRING MY BABY BACK TO LIFE
OR ELSE."
And Shiva is like "Or else what?"
And Parvati's like "Or else I'm gonna turn into Kali
and you're gonna have to chase me down
and dance me into submission again."
And Shiva is like "Hmm. Good point."

So Shiva sends out some of his dudes
to go grab the first head they find
and bring it back to him
and I guess he has pretty dumb servants
because they come back with the head of an
     ELEPHANT
and Shiva is like "Guys
I feel like it would have been easier to just decapitate
     a baby
rather than a full-grown elephant
and also you should have figured out from context
     clues what I meant.
But whatever, I guess I'll make it work."
So he just glues this elephant head onto the dead baby
and that somehow causes it to come back to life
and that is why Ganesh has an elephant head now
and also why he is the god of wisdom
which is bad news for Shiva

because an elephant
NEVER FORGETS.

So the moral of the story
is that you shouldn't worry if you accidentally kill
    your baby
just kill another baby and glue pieces of it to the first
    baby until it comes back to life.
Works every time
or at least
this one time.

JAPANESE

ARE YOU READY
FOR DISTENDED RACCOON TESTICLES?
NO?
WELL, YOU BETTER GET READY QUICK
BECAUSE JAPAN JUST CALLED
AND IT'S 'BOUT TO DELIVER ONE WHOPPER
    OF A BALLSACK TO THE BRAINPAN.
I think you may find it comforting to know
that Japan was no less strange two thousand years ago
than it is today
they did not have the technology
to build flying boobs and hand-job robots
but weird shit has always been Japan's prime natural
    resource
as the thousand-plus deities in the Shinto pantheon
can proudly attest
so have a seat
get comfortable
but I cannot assure you
that what you are sitting on
is not a raccoon's nuts.

◆ ◆ ◆

IZANAMI GETS REAL SORE

So where do we begin?
Oh, I know
HOW ABOUT THE BEGINNING?
DURRRR.

Okay, so apparently there's like a hojillion generations
    of gods in Japan.
In fact, there are so many generations
that it takes seven of them JUST TO GET US TO
    THE DUDES WHO CREATE THE EARTH.
What the hell were those other generations of gods
    doing?
Just havin' orgies
not messing with ANY MORTALS AT ALL?
That . . . sounds pretty ideal, actually.

Anyway, after seven generations
we finally get our two main characters:
Izanagi (meaning "he who invites")
and Izanami (meaning "SHE who invites")
(that has nothing to do with how they behave
or who they are or anything.
It's not like the entirety of creation is a fancy dinner
    party.
Just thought it would be a nice detail to include.)
Izanagi and Izanami are probably siblings
based on how similar their names are.

(See also: Tweedledee and Tweedledum)
And seeing as this is mythology
their first act is to be like "HEY:
I MIGHT LIKE YOU BETTER IF WE SLEPT
    TOGETHER.
LET'S LEGITIMIZE IT WITH MARRIAGE!"
But since all the gods have just been chilling out
having nothing but orgies for millennia
no one even knows how marriage WORKS
so Izanagi and Izanami have to make it up from
    scratch
and what they come up with actually makes a lot of
    sense:
Izanagi's like "All right
what I'm gonna do is I'm gonna see you
and get REEEEALLY EXCITED
and then you are also gonna get REALLY EXCITED
and then we'll be married!"
And Izanami is like "Sounds great!
I mean, normally women are supposed to be super
    passive and not speak unless spoken to
but I guess I will make an exception in this case
because, bro
I am dying to get my bone on with you, bro."

So they do their crazy marriage thing
and then immediately get down to business
and then suddenly Izanami gives birth
to a hideous mutant leech baby.
BIG SURPRISE, ASSHOLES.
Y'ALL ARE SIBLINGS.
Actually, I want to go ahead and applaud the Japanese
for having the first mythos
that accurately portrays the outcome of incest.
Oh wait
I spoke too soon.

Turns out they had a leechbaby because Izanami
    TALKED DURING THE WEDDING.
WOMEN AREN'T SUPPOSED TO TALK, GUYS.
IT'S UNLADYLIKE, AND THEY WILL BE
    PUNISHED WITH LEECHES.
So they take a mulligan on the marriage
and this time Izanami keeps her fat mouth shut
and then they get bizzay
and give birth to
THE ISLAND OF JAPAN.
OW.
Not only is that not a living thing
thus making it even more mutant status than the
    leechbaby
but just imagine trying to push Japan out your
    ladyhole.
Izanami just gets all kinds of screwed over in this
    story.
Oh, I forgot to say
they bone so hard in the water that they create bubbles
and the bubbles
turn into all the other landmasses on Earth
which is good
because it means Izanami doesn't have to individually
    birth EVERY SINGLE OTHER PLACE
but even so
Japan is not the last-level hazard Izanami has to scooch
    out her cooch.
Enter (or rather exit) KAGUTSUCHI
GOD OF FIRE.
OWWWW.
This is disgusting, guys.
I am disgusted.
Oh, and that's finally what kills Izanami
so now she's dead
but it's okay

(kind of)
because when Izanami dies
a whole bunch of other gods fly out of her corpse
like the god of earth and stuff
and then Izanagi starts crying about it
and his tears turn into MORE GODS
and then he gets pissed off
and cuts Kagutsuchi into pieces
and guess what the pieces turn into
DING DING DING
MORE GODS.
Is there anything anyone can do in ancient Japan
that does not result in more gods?
Answer: no.

So then Izanami calms down a little bit
(he is cycling through the stages of grief mighty fast)
and he decides to go down to Yomi
which is Japanese hell
and try and get her back.
So he goes down there and finds Izanami
and he's like "'Sup, gurl
wanna come be alive with me again or something?"
And Izanami is like "Aw shit, bro
I already ate a bunch of pomegranates or whatever
and now I can't leave.
Here, let me introduce you to my friend Persephone.
I understand she has had the EXACT SAME
          EXPERIENCE IN ANOTHER COUNTRY."

So Izanagi is pretty disappointed
but he decides to chill out in Yomi for a while anyway
except here's the problem
at some point he lights a torch
and he sees his wife

and she appears to have traded in her hotness
for a lifetime supply of MAGGOTS
and he's like "AW HELL NO, GIRL
I was gonna ask about conjugal visits in hell
but I think I need to change my mind
BECAUSE IT JUST SHAT ITSELF WITH
    HORROR."
And Izanami is like "Come back, bro, don't be a pussy."
And Izanagi is like "HIGGITY-HELL NO."
And Izanami is like "Fine, dick.
How about I kill a thousand people a day for the rest of
    eternity?"
And Izanagi is like "Okay, you do that.
I will create ONE THOUSAND AND FIVE
    HUNDRED people every day.
Suck it, uggo.
Or actually, don't suck it.
I don't want to come down with a case of maggot
    dong."

So I guess they probably have a bidding war for a while
where Izanami ups the number of dudes she kills
and Izanagi ups the number of dudes he makes
and they keep doing that basically forever, as far as I
    can tell
and that's where overpopulation comes from!

So the moral of the story
is that access to safe and effective birth control
should be a human right
because no woman
should ever have to give birth
to Japan.

◆ ◆ ◆

Susanoo Has No Idea
What He's Doing

So I don't know whose bright idea it was to have
    storm gods
but these guys are nothing but problems.
We've got Zeus for starters
(I don't even wanna open that can of philandering
    worms right now)
and then there's Thor
world-champion ruckus causer
but as if those two problem machines weren't enough
we also have one of the ultimate prodigies
of irrational sex and violence.
Ladies and gentlemen, allow me to present to you:
SUSANOO

Now I know what you're thinking
you're thinking that SUSANOO sounds like an
    overacted exclamation from a bad soap opera.
My friends, I assure you that it is not.
It is actually the name of the Japanese god of storms
birthed by Izanagi one day
when he was washing his nose.
So one day Susanoo gets kicked out of heaven
for being too rowdy
and on his way out he goes to say good-bye to his sister
    Amaterasu.
Now, Susanoo and Amaterasu are not on the best of
    terms

so Amaterasu thinks her bro might be trying to play
    one last prank on her on his way out
but Susanoo is like "No, sis, I just wanna say good-bye.
Here, let me prove my sincerity to you
by engaging you in a VERY WEIRD CONTEST."
So what they do
is they each pick an inanimate object
and see how many gods they can make the object give
    birth to
because in ancient Japan
causing unlikely things to give birth
is a time-honored tradition.
In fact, having babies the normal way
is considered kinda gauche.
So Amaterasu picks Susanoo's sword
and she makes it give birth to three chicks
and meanwhile Susanoo is using his sister's necklace
to make five dudes
and then Susanoo is like "Well, I guess I win
because my sword was what gave birth to chicks
and chicks are worth double points."
And for some reason they don't argue over this at all
and everything is great.

BUT NOT FOR LONG
because seeing as he is the god of storms
it takes all of six seconds
for Susanoo to start making bad decisions.
Everyone is basically just going around
minding their own business
when WHAM WHAM WIMMY WOZZLE
here comes Susanoo, shitting on everybody's rice fields
then he cuts up a pony
and throws it at his sister's loom
and then kills one of her attendants
for no good reason.

Basically you can tell he didn't spend very long
    planning this rampage
but even so, it ends up being so horrible that his sister
    crawls into a cave and refuses to come out.

So of course now he gets exiled for REAL
and on the way out
he figures he should get some groceries
so he hits up the food goddess for some food
and she hooks him up with all kinds of stuff
but apparently she is taking all of this stuff out of really
    gross places on her body
and Susanoo is not okay with that
so he kills her.
GREAT JOB, DICK.
WHERE IS ALL THE FOOD GONNA COME
    FROM NOW?
But it's okay
because since she is the food goddess
her whole dead body immediately turns into food
so like
silkworms come out of her head
and rice comes out of her eyes
and small beans come out of her nose
and millet comes out of her ears
and barley shoots out of her junk
and then large beans come out of her fundament
which is what my sourcebook seems to think a butt is
    called.

So that all turns out okay
but now Susanoo is FOR REAL TRIPLE EXILED
So he's wandering around down on Earth
when he sees this man and woman
crying all over their daughter
and he's like "Whoa, whoa, stop that.

What's going on?"
And they're like "Well, see
we used to have eight daughters
but every year for the last seven years
one of our daughters has been eaten
by the YAMATA NO OROCHI."
And Susanoo is like "Uhh, what is that?"
And they're like "WELL.
It's a snake
but instead of one head, it has eight
and instead of one tail, it has eight
and instead of being normal snake size
it is as long as eight hills and eight valleys.
ARE YOU BEGINNING TO NOTICE A THEME?
Also, moss grows on its back
and its eyes are like cherries
I don't know how the world turtle and Santa Claus got
    mixed in here
but HOLY CANNOLI THIS THING IS SCARY."
And Susanoo is like "Pshaw, my friends
I am your local god of storms
romping and stomping is what I DO.
How about you let me have your daughter
and I will kill this big snake?"
And the parents
(who are names are Foot-Stroker and Hand-Stroker)
are like "Okay, sure, sweet."
So immediately Susanoo goes WAZZAP KAGOW
and turns the daughter
(whose name is Beautiful-Rice-Field-Princess)
into a comb
which he immediately stuffs in his hair
presumably to keep her safe
but more likely because he has no idea how sex actually
    works.

We are talking about guy who has made a career
out of forcing necklaces to give birth.
And then he's like "ALL RIGHT, GUYS
HERE'S THE PLAN:
I need you to build eight gates
and eight pedestals to put behind the eight gates
and I want you to make eight pots
full of booze that has been distilled EIGHT TIMES
because we're kind of on a roll with the whole eight thing
and then I want you to set that all up for me
and we should be good."
So they set all that stuff up
and pretty soon the snake comes along
and it smells the octuple-distilled booze and it is like
"OH DAMN
LOOKS LIKE SOMEONE IS HAVING A PARTY.
TIME TO TRANSFER THE ENTIRE LIQUOR
    CONTENT OF THAT PARTY INTO MY
    BODY."
Which is basically what I yell every time I show up to a
    party.
But yeah, the snake gets absolutely trashed in all eight
    of its heads
and then they passes out
at which point Susanoo just strolls by
idly decapitating each of the heads in succession
except he only gets halfway
when his sword hits something and
    TOTALLY BREAKS.
Oh wait, it's fine.
It turns out what he broke his sword on
is just A BRAND-NEW SWORD
so it looks like it all worked out in the end.
Pretty soon after that
they let him back into heaven

because who is going to argue with a guy
who just decapitated a snake eight times?

So the moral of the story
is that no matter what shape or size
drunk animals are ALWAYS hilarious.

✦ ✦ ✦

AMATERASU AND THE
CRIPPLING DEPRESSION

So, Amaterasu is hiding in a cave.
She is doing this because this is what you do when
    your brother is the god of storms
and he does things like tear up ponies
and shit in rice fields for absolutely no reason.
This is a problem.
This is a problem because Amaterasu is the sun
and the sun is important for things, like
for example
organic life.
But no one can talk Amaterasu out of her sadhole
no matter how many funny voices they do
and the gods are all starting to get pretty nervous
because how are they going to have sweet beach
    parties without the sun?
So they have a big meeting of all the gods
and that is quite a thing
because there are about EIGHT HUNDRED GODS.
Yeah

Shintos don't mess around.
And all of these gods sit down
and they start brainstorming
and I don't think they ever got more than halfway
    through brainstorming
because here is what they end up doing:

They get a mirror
and a giant necklace
and some cherry bark
and they put it on some tree they found
and then they get this chick named Ama-no-Uzumi
whose name means
"DREAD CELESTIAL FEMALE"
to do a silly dance on a washtub
until everybody is just laughing their holy asses off.
Okay, so far it sounds like a pretty good party
but where does the plan come in?
Well, see, what happens
is that Amaterasu hears everybody having a good time
and she comes out of her cave
like "Hey wait, why is everybody so happy?
Last thing I remember
some dude was chucking dead horses through
    everything."
And all the other gods are like "Oh
we are SO over that now.
Now we are all about this new goddess we found.
She is SOOOO much prettier than you it is amazing.
Look, check it out."
And then they hold up the mirror
and Amaterasu thinks that her reflection
is a DIFFERENT PERSON.
You heard it here first, my friends
the sun is on the same level intellectually
as that puppy you had when you were five

you know
the one that kept beating its head against the hall
    mirror because it was trying to play with itself.

So Amaterasu is so into her own radiant glory
that she can't stop herself from walking toward the
    mirror
and meanwhile some other gods are creeping along
    behind her
roping off her escape route
so she HAS to go back into the sky
and then she does
and everyone is free to get as many sunburns as they
    can handle.

So the moral of the story
is don't wear reflective clothing
because the sun will think you are her
and then she will incinerate you while trying to make
    your acquaintance.

❖ ❖ ❖

Tanukis Have Big Balls

So tanukis:
First of all, tanukis are a type of animal
that is as adorable as a bullet train full of kittens
(assuming that conveying things at high speed makes
    them more adorable).
Second of all
they are a cross between raccoons and dogs

making them utterly terrifying ur-bastards of the
highest caliber.
Third of all, they have
the BIGGEST TESTICLES POSSIBLE.
This is not a metaphor.
These dudes were rooting through the bargain bin at
Balls City
where they unearthed a whole case
of super deluxe triple XL men-tronomes
and then proceeded to use the ungodly influx of
testosterone
to go EVERYWHERE
and cause ALL THE PROBLEMS.
Seriously, the Japanese cannot stop making statues of
these little jerks
getting wrecked in straw hats
then dropping ludicrously ill beats
drummed out on their DISTENDED MANBULGES.
Think I'm making this up?
I dare you to put down this book right now
and go look up "tanuki testicles" on Google image
search.
Yep
those guys on the second row are using their balls to
bludgeon large fish to death.
You're welcome.

BUT YOU DID NOT BUY THIS BOOK TO
HEAR ME WAX POETIC ABOUT RACCOON
BALLS
(or if you did
then you have oddly specific taste in literature.)
So here is a myth about a tanuki:

Okay, so a tanuki gets married to a fox
and they have a baby

but they are having problems finding food
because their forest is WAYYY overhunted.
And they're about to starve to death
when the tanuki is suddenly like "Oh wait
we have magical shape-shifting powers.
Man, it is so great being a mythological creature."
So the fox shape-shifts into a dude
and the tanuki shape-shifts into a dead tanuki
and the fox carries the tanuki into town and is like
"Hey, guys, who wants to buy a tanuki?"
And everyone is like "I WILL GIVE YOU A
    HUNDRED BUCKS FOR THAT TESTICLE
    DOG."
And the fox is like "SOLD."
Then she uses the money to go buy a ton of food
and meanwhile the tanuki escapes from the house of
    the dude that bought him and goes home.

But one of the sucky things about food
is that it gets eaten and then it turns into poop
and so eventually they need to come up with a plan to
    get more food.
So the fox is like "All right, well
I should probably be the dead body this time
because it would be kinda suspicious if I walked into
    town again and tried to sell the same tanuki."
So the tanuki turns into a peasant dude
and the fox turns into a dead fox
and the tanuki carries the fox into town.
But oh no
it looks like some of those leviathan testicle veins
have burrowed into the tanuki's skull
because this is the point
where his balls seize control of his entire brain
and start hammering on the button marked "BAD
    DECISIONS."

See, he gets into town and he negotiates a sale
and then he's like "You know
one of the bad things about a wife
is you have to share food with her
so how about I tell the dude I'm selling my wife to
that she's still alive
and then he'll kill her and I'll live happily ever after!"
So he does that terrible thing
and the guy kills the fox with a brick
and then the tanuki celebrates his newfound
    bachelorhood by going out and getting TRASHED
and he stumbles back home to his son at like three a.m.
and the kid is like "Hey, Dad
what happened to mom?"
And the tanuki is like "Uh, well
whatever it was, it definitely had nothing to do with me
    purposefully getting her bricked to death."
And the kid is like "Uh, sure."

But as the days go by
the kid starts to get more and more suspicious
and also the tanuki is being a huge dick
and not sharing any food with him
so he's really got no love for this dude whatsoever
and finally one day he's like "Yo, Dad
you know mom taught me all her magical secrets
    before she died?"
And the tanuki is like "Bullshit. Prove it."
And the kid is like "Okay.
How about you go to a bridge in the forest
and I will shape-shift into something
and try to cross the bridge
and if you can recognize me, you win."
and the tanuki is like "YOU'RE ON, SON."
So he goes to this bridge in the middle of the woods
and a few minutes later his son shows up

but his son doesn't cross the bridge.
He just chills out by the far end of the bridge
and waits for his dad to screw himself
and sure enough, here comes the local king
on his chariot of jewels and human misery
and the tanuki is like "HAHAHA, NICE TRY, SON.
YOU THOUGHT I WOULDN'T RECOGNIZE YOU
AS A PROCESSION OF NOBLEMEN AND ALSO
    A CHARIOT.
ALLOW ME TO RUN UP AND PUNCH YOU IN
    THE FACE."
And the king is like "Okay, why is a raccoon dog trying
    to blackjack me with his ballsack?
Guards, I believe you are trained to handle wild
    animals and their comically large genitals?"
And the guards are like "SIR YES SIR."
And they throw the tanuki into the river
where he proceeds to die like a chump.
After that, I guess the kid starves to death
because he just killed his only surviving family
    member
and now who is he going to pretend to sell to the
    villagers?

So the moral of the story
is that although the temptation may be great
you should not assume that everybody you meet is a
    shape-shifter.
It is almost as dangerous as not assuming everyone
    you meet is a shape-shifter.

AFRICAN

Okay, so Africa
it's a big place
full of a lot of dudes with a lot of myths
so it's not like there is this big established canon
of pure uncut AFRICAN MYTHOLOGY
more like there's a bunch of little African mythologies
scattered all over the place
but like every single one of my girlfriends has told me
with a smile and a pat on the back
"It's not the size that matters
but if you ARE gonna have a tiny penis, you gotta at
    least be really freaky in bed to make up for it."
Uh
anyway
what I'm trying to say is that I can't tell all the myths
    from all the mythologies here
so I'm just gonna pick all the sweetest ones
in order to give you what I hope is a balanced picture
of what I think is the main through-line
of African mythology:
ordinary dudes
making ordinary mistakes
except those ordinary dudes happen to be gods so then
    there's problems.

Obatala Has a
Drinking Problem

So there's this dude Obatala.
He's one of the *orisha*
which are basically a bunch of gods
that exploded out of some other god's corpse
when one of his slaves dropped a big rock on him.
So, already this story is shaping up to be pretty sweet
but then it hits a major roadblock real fast:
Obatala wants to make a world
but he has NO IDEA HOW TO DO IT.
Frankly, I find the realism in this myth to be highly
      refreshing.
I mean, can any of us honestly say we know the first
      thing about creating a world?
Oh, look at me, I'm Ra
let me just will myself into being out of nothing
and then create land
with nothing but my left nut and
PURE GUMPTION.
NO.
THAT'S NOT HOW THIS WORKS.
You have to SIT YOUR ASS DOWN
and you have to BRAINSTORM.

So that's what Obatala does.
He hits up his buddy Olorun, the sky god
and he's like "Yo, Olorun
I wanna make a world with some people in it."

and Olorun, who is the king of the gods
is like "Oh man, that sounds great
but it also sounds REALLY HARD.
Do you have any plans?
Like some blueprints or something?"
And Obatala is like "Uhh . . .
I'll get back to you."

So at this point Obatala really only has one option
and that is to go see Orunmila, their resident fortune-
    teller.
So Obatala goes over to Orunmila's house
and Orunmila is like "Duuuude!
I can totally tell you how to make a world.
Let's go into my back room
and stare at my nuts for a while."
(He tells fortunes by throwing palm nuts and reading
    their patterns
but I failed to clarify that because I was looking for an
    excuse to write "stare at my nuts.")
So after peering intently into his nuts for a while
Orunmila is like "All right, dude
here's what you gotta do:
Step one
descend down to Earth
on a GOLD CHAIN ATTACHED TO THE SKY.
Oh man
that would make such a sweet album cover.
Uh, uh . . . STEP TWO!
Go down to Earth carrying a hen, a black cat
a palm nut, and a snail shell full of sand."
And Obatala is like "What?"
And Orunmila is like "What?
Sorry, dude, I'm pretty high right now."

But it's not like Obatala has any better ideas

so he goes about trying to make this ultimate gold
    chain
but he doesn't have NEARLY enough gold
so he gives the gold he DOES have to the celestial
    goldsmith
and then he goes all over the sky, collecting
    investors.
He's like "GUYS
GUYS.
Have I got a deal for YOU!
So I don't know if you've noticed
but there's a whole world of untapped real estate
down underneath this sky place.
Why, I ask you
are we totally underutilizing this prime acreage
when AS WE SPEAK
dudes could be down there *CAUSING PROBLEMS*??
Think about it
a whole world full of wretched, fleshy problem
    machines
for you to set on fire and put your dicks in."
And all the gods are like "SIGN ME UP."

So Obatala goes back to the jewel smith
with a big sack full of gold
but it STILL won't quite reach the Earth
so Obatala is just like "Screw it, man
just make it as long as you can.
I'll figure something out.
There's gotta be some reason I exploded out of my
    dad's corpse, right?"
And then he takes the chicken, the cat, the palm nut
and the snail shell full of sand
and he starts climbing down to Earth.
I am kinda curious where he got the chicken and
    stuff from

seeing as there is not really any land
or animal life or anything
but I'll let it slide.
THIS TIME.

So he gets down to the bottom of the chain
and he can't quite reach the dim, watery morass that
    is the whole world
so he's trying to figure out what to do
when here comes Orunmila's voice from the sky
like "Duuuude:
Empty out that snail shell."
So he does, and the sand falls down below him
and it makes some land
and then Orunmila is like "Duuuude:
Drop your chicken on the sand."
You know what this feels like?
This feels like one of those adventure games
where you spend like seventeen hours
wandering around the haunted mansion
with a backpack full of junk and a heart full of fury
because you didn't think to stuff the pigeon in the
    jukebox or something.
Like, how was Obatala supposed to figure this
    shit out?
But anyway, he drops the chicken
and the chicken kicks the sand all over the place
and it turns into all the land
and then Obatala drops down there with the cat
but then he's totally out of ideas
so he just kinda sits there and waits for something to
    happen.

About a week later
Olorun sends one of his dudes to see what's up
and Obatala is like "Man, I dunno.

This seemed like a great idea, but it's really dark down
      here and I'm starting to lose motivation."
So this message gets passed along to Olorun
who is just like "Oh, no problem. Boom."
And he makes the sun.
Are you telling me this dude knew how to make the
      sun all along
but couldn't figure out how to populate the damn
      Earth?
Well, whatever.
What's important is that Obatala gets super jazzed by
      all the sunlight
and he plants that palm nut
and it turns into a palm tree
and then he decides to make a bunch of humans out
      of clay
because he forgot that that was why he came down
      here in the first place.
So he's working on the hot sun
sculpting all these dudes
and he gets pretty thirsty
so he starts drinking some palm wine
because it's not like he's SURROUNDED BY WATER
      or anything.
So he's sculpting all the dudes
and drinking all the wine
and by the time he's sculpted the last dude
he is so tipsy he is basically like a one-man teeter-totter
like if he were to breathe into a Breathalyzer
the BREATHALYZER would get drunk.
Dude is triggity-trashed, is what I am trying to say.

So Obatala goes and passes out
and sleeps off all that wine
and when he wakes up
he goes to admire all the dudes he made

but he notices that some of the dudes got a little
    messed up
because he was so totally plastered when he was
    molding them.
Actually, they're more than a little messed up
because this is where shit like POLIO and
    BLINDNESS comes from.
Great job, Lushy McDrunkenstein
you invented birth defects.
Huzzah!

But to his credit
Obatala does feel REALLY bad about all this
and I don't know whether it's his guilt
or the WICKED hangover he must be dealing with
but he is like "Ugh
I am NEVER drinking again."
And then he doesn't
and he also devotes his life to helping crippled dudes
so I guess it turns out okay.

So the moral of the story
is that if you die and it turns out reincarnation exists
try to come back as a cat
because that little bastard got a free pass to Earth
and he didn't have to do SHIT.

◆ ◆ ◆

Local Father Discovers Immortality with This One Weird Tip!

One day Anansi the Ashanti spider-man is dicking
　　around in the wilderness outside his town
and he gets bored and thirsty
and he sees this house with an old man sitting on the
　　porch.
Now, when I say old
I mean OLLLLD
this guy makes the Crypt Keeper look like Natalie
　　fucking Portman.
So Anansi walks up to this old man
and he's like "Excuse me, you fugly sonofabitch
can I get some ice-cold drinking water?"
And the old man doesn't say anything.
So Anansi is like
"I said: CAN I GET SOME ICY COLD WATER
　　PRODUCT UP IN HERE?"
And the old man says nothing.
So Anansi is like "Please continue sitting motionless if
　　you want me to go inside and raid your fridge."
And the old man says nothing
so Anansi goes inside and has a gay old time.
He has such a gay time that he comes back the next day
and the next day
just straight up pillaging this dude's pantry.
And I don't know what this dude has in his pantry

but whatever it is, it must be pretty good
'cause one day Anansi brings his eldest daughter with
    him to the house
and he is like "Thank you so much for all this free food,
    creepy silent old guy.
To thank you, here is my eldest daughter.
You guys are married now. Have fun.
Also, daughter?
Go inside and make me a sandwich."
And then he eats the sandwich
and leaves his daughter and goes home.

So the next day he goes back for more free food
and maybe to see his daughter, I guess.
But his daughter isn't there.
WHERE DID SHE GO?
He knows she likes to play hide-and-seek
so he starts looking all over the house
and finally he goes and looks in the last possible place
THE OVEN
and what does he find in there?
THE WEDDING RING HE GAVE HIS
    DAUGHTER.
So he runs outside to the old man like "HEY
ASSHOLE
WHY DID YOU TAKE OFF MY DAUGHTER'S
    WEDDING RING?
SHIT WAS EXPENSIVE."
And the old man FINALLY starts talking.
He's all "Do you know who I am?
I'm Death.
You showed up at my house
you ate all my food
and then you married me to a gross ugly spider chick
without my consent
so I ATE YOUR DAUGHTER

and now I am also going to eat YOU."
And Anansi is like "No no no.
I like not having consequences for my actions.
This seems like a consequence. This is terrible."

So he starts running.
He figures Death is probably pretty slow
given how old he is
but no, he's keeping up
and Anansi starts getting tired, so he climbs a tree
and he's about to jump to another tree
when he looks down
and sees Death just standing there
because guess what, guys:
DEATH CANNOT CLIMB TREES.
I guess this explains why squirrels are immortal?
So the personification of death itself
is just standing at the bottom of this tree
and he starts chucking everything in arm's reach at
    Anansi
and eventually he runs out of shit to throw
and goes to find more shit
at which point Anansi jumps out of the tree
and books it for his house, screaming "HEY, HEY
WIFE AND KIDS:
CLIMB UP TO THE CEILING
DEATH IS COMING.
MY WILD IRRESPONSIBLITY HAS ONCE
    AGAIN ENDANGERED MY ENTIRE
    FAMILY
AM I, PERHAPS
THE BEST HUSBAND AND FATHER?"
And his wife is like
"WHAT'S THAT?
I CANT HEAR YOU OVER THE SOUND OF OUR
    FOUR STARVING CHILDREN

STUCK HERE ALL DAY WHILE YOU RAID
    DEATH'S KITCHEN FOR YOURSELF."
And Anansi is like "FINE. I'll take them up to the
    ceiling MYSELF."
So he runs into the house
and drags everybody up to the ceiling
and Death runs in after him
and sees everyone up on the ceiling
and he can't do a thing about it
except pull up a chair
grab a burlap sack
and just sit there
waiting.

So it's not too long before Anansi's youngest son starts
    losing his grip on the ceiling.
Wait. Since when has a spider had ceiling problems?
Spiders LIVE on my fucking ceiling.
THEY WON'T LEAVE.
The only explanation is that these spiders are like . . .
    reverse Spider-Man
with all the disadvantages of a spider
coupled with all the disadvantages of a man.
So anyway, this kid is like "DADDY, HELP!"
And Anansi is like "HOLD ON, JUNIOR.
IF YOU FALL, DEATH WILL EAT YOU."

So Junior falls
and Death catches him
and is like "I'm only after your dad, kid.
But I'm still gonna stick you in this burlap sack."
Then Anansi's youngest daughter falls off
and the same thing happens
and again and again
until it's just Anansi up there

and he's about to lose his grip
when he goes "WAIT!
DEATH!
I am SOOOO FAT
from eating SOOO MUCH OF YOUR FOOD.
If I fall to the floor
I'm totally going to explode on impact
and then what are you gonna eat?
Spider guts?
Gross.
What you SHOULD do
is go get my big barrel of flour from the kitchen
and put it under me
so that when I fall, you get a nice breading on me."
So Death is like "Dur, okay.
Just let me leave you alone in the room real quick."
And Anansi is like "YESSSS.
Man, I am such a genius. Holy shit!
I can't believe I have LITERALLY CHEATED
        DEATH with my sheer genius!"
But by the time Anansi is done congratulating himself
Death has come back in with the barrel
and Anansi is like "Balls."
But all is not lost
because when Death leans over the barrel
to make sure it's centered
Anansi drops down on the back of his head
which freaks him out
because, you know
spider on his head
and in the resulting confusion and flour-induced
        blindness
Anansi is able to grab his wife and kids
and run out the door
and he's been escaping Death ever since.

Actually, that's why those spiders won't leave my
  ceiling.
It's because Death still hasn't figured out how to use
  ladders.

So now you know, guys.
The secret to immortality
is to duct tape yourself to the ceiling

You're welcome.

◆ ◆ ◆

ESHU ELEGBA IS PROBABLY THE LAST DUDE YOU WANT APPROVING YOUR FRIENDSHIP

Okay, so there's this dude Eshu Elegba, right?

He's one of the main gods in the Yoruba pantheon
and also a pretty crazy dude.
Basically, he is what it would be like
if Loki was pretty much allowed to run his whole
  pantheon.
He is associated mainly with roads, trickery, pipe-
  smoking, and dongs.
The last two may be interrelated.
Hell, the last three.

You know what?
Everything is related to dongs.
MOVING ON.

So there are these two farmers.
They are best buds, and they live across the street from
    each other.
So one day they're sitting out on their respective
    porches
enjoying the sunshine and each others' companionship
when Eshu Elegba walks by real fast
and the farmer on the north side of the road is like
"Dude, did you see that guy just now?
The one with the red hat?"
and the farmer on the south side of the street is like
"Uh, I saw a guy
but he was wearing a BLUE AND WHITE hat.
I think maybe you've had too much to drink."
And the first farmer is like "Guess again, shit eyes.
That guy's hat was clearly red."
And the second farmer is like "YOU are the one with
    shit for eyes."
And the first farmer is like "I'LL SHIT IN YOUR
    EYES."
And just then, Eshu Elegba walks past in the other
    direction
and the first farmer is like "Holy balls, you're right.
The dude's hat IS blue and white."
And the second guy is like "What are you talking
    about?
YOU are the one who is right.
That guy's hat is CLEARLY red."
And the first farmer is like
"YOU KNOW WHAT'S RED?
MY FIST

AFTER I USE IT TO RIP YOUR STILL-BEATING
    HEART FROM YOUR CHEST."
And the other guy is all "NOT AS RED AS HIS HAT,
    YOU SHANDY-PANCAKE."
and the first guy is like "WHAT THE HELL IS A
    SHANDY-PANCAKE?"
and the second guy is like "I DON'T HAVE TO
    KNOW WHAT IT IS
TO CUT YOUR FACE OFF WITH IT."
And then the neighbors show up like "Okay, guys,
enough is enough.
We're gonna take you both to the king
and let him sort it out."

So they go all the way to the king
and they get into the throne room
and then Eshu shows up
like "POOF KLAZAM, DICKHEADS."
And they see his hat from the front
because I guess they never tried to look at him
while he was RUNNING TOWARD OR AWAY
    FROM THEM
and WHAT DO YOU KNOW:
IT'S HALF RED AND HALF WHITE/BLUE
IT IS BASICALLY THE ULTIMATE U.S.A. PARTY
    FEDORA
and Elegba is like "Guess what, guys:
YOU JUST GOT PUNK'D.
This is what happens when you make a new friend
without consulting me first
BECAUSE I'M ELEGBA
APPROVER OF FRIENDSHIPS.
JK, guys, I actually just kinda wanted to see a fight.
CAUSING STRIFE IS MY GREATEST JOY."
And then he runs off and everyone is like "Wow.
Who put that dude in charge of the universe?"

Which is a question I think has been asked many times
about pretty much every god.

So the moral of the story
is make sure to eat your carrots
because good eyesight may just save your friendship.

CHINESE

So considering how the current official religion of
    China
seems to be something like "Stand still while we
    bulldoze your house to build this dam"
it's hard to put a finger
on the relationship between ancient Chinese tales
and any specific religion.
In fact
the way it really works
is that wayyy back in the day, some dudes got together
and made up some sweet stories
but they kinda forgot to attach a religion to them
so then later on, all these other religions came along
like Taoism and Confucianism and Buddhism
they were all like "Whoa, these myths are pretty sweet!
Let's steal them!"
So all the tropes of the old myths got repurposed
to make the points of all these new religions
and meanwhile
a whole bunch of the old myths made it through
more or less intact
so in this section
I'm gonna try to give you a little taste
of all the different religions
that bastardized Chinese mythology
just like I'm about to.

◆ ◆ ◆

Pan Gu Is a Pretty Big Dude

Okay, so Pan Gu, right?
Apparently he was a dude living inside an egg back in
    the day.
Where was the egg, you ask?
Probably in China
because that is where this myth is from.
BZZ
WRONG.
CHINA DOESN'T EXIST YET IN THIS STORY.
THIS IS A CREATION MYTH
TRY TO KEEP UP.

Actually this egg is pretty much all there is anywhere
and inside the egg is all this cool stuff
like lava and birds and mountains and boobs
and also this dude Pan Gu, like I said.
But even though Pan Gu literally has access to
    EVERYTHING THERE IS
he gets pretty bored inside this egg
and he's like "OKAY, THAT'S ENOUGH."
and he picks up an ax and breaks that egg in half
LIKE A BOSS.
Then he proceeds to have an EIGHTEEN-
    THOUSAND-YEAR growth spurt
constantly holding the top of the egg balanced on his
    head in the process

which basically turns the top of the egg into the sky
and the bottom into the earth.
It is very important that Pan Gu maintain proper
    posture
because otherwise we're all pooched.

But so yeah
then his beard turns into forests and whatnot.
I think his bone marrow turns into rubies also
and something about his breath and wind and birds.
Whatever.
This dude is literally everything
so you can kind of assume that if there is a thing
it probably came about
as a result of one of Pan Gu's bodily processes.
But the best part is where humans come from
because apparently
humans are the lice that come off this dude's corpse
when he dies.
Yep
we are all lice, ladies and gentlemen.

So the moral of the story is
never bathe
because it is genocide.

CHANG'E IS A
SUBSTANCE ABUSER

Okay, so you guys know about the sun, right?

It's this big ball of fire and explosions
that flies around giving people cancer.
But did you know there used to be TEN SUNS?
Yeah
it SUCKED.
It sucked so bad that Di Jun (aka Chinese Zeus)
(aka the father of all these rambunctious suns)
(Get it? Suns? Sons? It's brilliant.)
had no idea what to do
so here's what went down:

There's this really great archer named Hou Yi
and he's chilling in his heavenly crib
with his wife Chang'e
and all of a sudden the phone rings and it's Di Jun.
Hou Yi is like "Yo, Di Jun, my man, what's cookin'?"
And Di Jun is like "My friend
the entire Earth is cooking.
You could fry an egg on a goddamn glacier right
        about now
and it ain't none of this sous-vide bullshit or nothing.
This is honest-to-goodness
summer backyard barbecue
except instead of a big plate of watermelon on the back
        porch

everyone's skin is melting off.
Can you solve this problem for me?"
And Hou Yi is like "You got it, buddy."
So Hou Yi grabs his trusty arrows and goes outside
and just kills nine out of the ten suns
and then he stares at the tenth sun real hard
and he's like
"You best behave, sun."
And the sun is like "OKAY DUDE, NO PROBLEM."
And promptly dives underground and takes the
    subway home
and Hou Yi is like "Well, that was easy.
You're welcome, Di Jun."
And Di Jun is like "WHAT THE HELL, DUDE
YOU JUST KILLED 90 PERCENT OF MY
    SUNS.
I MEAN SONS.
I MEAN TECHNICALLY BOTH, BUT
WHATEVER."
And Hou Yi is like "Dude, do you even know who you
    called to solve your problem?
You called Hou Yi the immortal archer.
And you know what they say:
When the only tool you have is a hammer
every problem starts to look like you can solve it by
    shooting your friend's sons.
Ummm, I think I may have mixed my metaphors a
    little bit."
And Di Jun is like "DAMN RIGHT YOU DID.
I AM HEREBY REVOKING YOUR
    IMMORTALITY.
ALSO:
YOUR WIFE'S IMMORTALITY."
And Chang'e is like "Wait, what did I do?"

So now Hou Yi and Chang'e are both mortal

and Chang'e will NOT stop bitching about it
for good reason.
So finally Hou Yi is like "GRR, FINE.
I will go get us some immortality."
So he goes all the way to the west
and he finds Xiwangmu, the good witch of the west
who gives him a couple pills of immortality
and she's like "Careful, dude.
This is some heavy shit.
Don't take too much."
And Hou Yi is like "Sure, no problem."
And then proceeds to go home
and leave all the pills with his wife
while he goes out to shoot more things with arrows.

Now, different tellers of this story ascribe different
    motivations to Chang'e here.
Some say she was a greedy twank who wanted all the
    immortality for herself.
Some say that there were some robbers and she took all
    the pills to spite them.
Some say she got hungry and confused.
Whatever the reason, the point is that Hou Yi isn't
    gone for fifteen seconds
before all the pills are in his wife's mouth
at which point she proceeds to have
THE ULTIMATE OVERDOSE.
But instead of throwing up and then dying
which would be SILLY
Chang'e becomes TOO IMMORTAL
and apparently immortality = buoyancy
so she floats to the moon
and her husband comes home
and sees her floating to the moon
and he's about to take out his bow
and try to shoot her down

but everyone is all "NO, HOU YI
SOMETIMES YOU CANNOT SOLVE PROBLEMS
    BY SHOOTING THEM."
And Hou Yi is like "Seriously?
Why did nobody tell me this before?"
and then his wife lives on the moon with a rabbit
    forever
and later another guy named Wu Gang gets sent there.
He's like Sisyphus except with a tree instead of a rock
and chopping it down instead of pushing it up a hill.

So the moral of the story
is don't do drugs
unless you wanna wake up on the moon
with nothing but a rabbit and a deranged lumberjack
    to keep you company.
Take it from me, man.

Take it from me.

◆ ◆ ◆

FEI CHANG-FANG
AND THE POOP MYSTIC

Okay, you are about to hear a story about magic
and poop
and I wish I could say that the magic was the most
    important part.

So Fei Chang-Fang is a dude who is interested in the
    Tao from a very early age

and then at a slightly less early age
he becomes a police officer
but then he quits because fuck the police.
So then one day he is hanging out at a restaurant
and he sees this old man
come walking into the town square
and the old man sits down
and pulls some medicinal herbs
(cough cough)
out of a large gourd
and proceeds to sell them all day.
Now Chang-Fang, having just quit his job
has nothing better to do than sit in the restaurant
and watch this dude sell drugs all day
and at the end of the day
the old dude puts all his herbs back into the gourd
and then SHOOP
jumps into the gourd himself
and Chang-Fang just sits there like
"what."

So he sits at the restaurant every day for a week,
watching this guy do this
and finally he's like "Screw it
I'm just gonna go talk to this dude."
So he gets up and walks across the courtyard
but right when he is about to get up in the old guy's
        business
the old guy goes SHOOP SHOOP BA-DOOP
and jumps into his gourd.
so Chang-Fang goes and looks in the gourd
and I will be DAMNED if there isn't an entire HOUSE
chilling out inside that gourd.
And the old dude is all up in there
and he walks right up to the mouth of the gourd
and looks Chang-Fang right in the eye

and is like "HOW DID YOU SEE ME GO INTO
    THE GOURD?
ONLY PEOPLE WHO CAN LEARN MAGIC CAN
    SEE ME GO INTO THE GOURD.
HERE. COME HAVE LUNCH IN MY GOURD."
So Chang-Fang jumps into the gourd with the old
    dude and they have a tasty lunch
and they have many tasty lunches for days afterward
and discuss the mysteries of the Tao.

But one day the old man in the gourd is like "Hey
Chang-Fang
I like how your name rhymes
and also I have a confession to make:
I am actually a Taoist immortal
imprisoned on earth for breaking the laws of heaven
they make me sell drugs down here
to atone for selling drugs up there.
Anyway, I get out tomorrow and I'm totally going back
    to the immortal kingdom.
Wanna come with?"
And Chang-Fang is like "DO I?
Oh wait, do I?"
'Cause, see, Chang-Fang has a family
and he doesn't want them to worry about him.
But the old dude is like "Boy
do I have a solution for THAT.
Here, take this bamboo stick
and hang it from a tree in front of your house."
So Chang-Fang does
and then his parents come outside
and they see the stick
only instead of a stick they see THEIR SON.
HE KILLED HIMSELF.
THEY ARE SO SAD.

And meanwhile Chang-Fang is standing next to them
like "Totally not dead, guys."
But they don't see or hear him
so the old man from the gourd is like "Welp
looks like I just destroyed your only reason for not
	coming with me."
And Chang-Fang is like "Checkmate, sir."
And they journey to the immortal mountains.

So the old man leads Chang-Fang into a cave
and makes him sit down on a slab of rock
and then he's like WAM BAM WIZZOW
and conjures a huge rock over Chang-Fang's head
suspended by a puny-ass rope
and then he's like FIZZANG PACHOW BLORB
and summons a bunch of snakes to bite the crap out of
	the rope
and the rope starts to fray
and Chang-Fang is just like "Yawn.
I see you have some snakerope.
Well done, I guess."

So the old man is like "NICE!
You are totally worthy to learn magic and divination."
And then he leads him up a mountain pass
and then he waves his hands
and ABRA-KA-GODDAMN-DABRA
IT'S POOPTIME
Seriously, there is just so much poop all of a sudden.
Just a massive pile of poops.
And do you know what it is covered in?
not marshmallows
or peanut brittle.
Nope
MAGGOTS

JUST A WHOOOOLE BUNCH OF MAGGOTS
and the old man grabs three maggots
and is like "Here, Chang-Fang.
Here are some maggots for you to eat."
And Chang-Fang is like "What? No."
And the old man is like "Aww, man.
I thought you were cool.
Looks like you don't get to be an immortal now."
And Chang-Fang is like "I guess I'm okay with that
if being an immortal
means I have to eat poop maggots.
Anyway, do you have any magic consolation prizes
     for me?"
And the old man is like "VANNA
TELL THE MAN WHAT HE'S WON."
And Vanna White doesn't say anything
because she's not there and the old man is crazy
so then he's just like "Well
you can have my gourd full of drugs
and you can have this magic teleporting walking stick.
GOOD-BYE
     I WILL NEVER SEE YOU AGAIN."

So then Chang-Fang kind of starts to wonder how his
     parents are doing
so he teleports home and knocks on his door
And his dad opens up the door like "OH NO
A GHOST."
But then Chang-Fang is like "Calm down, Dad.
I'm not a ghost.
I just pranked you into burying a bamboo stick using
     magic.
Here, I'll prove it."
So they go dig up the stick
and then everyone is happy again
and they have a banquet.

But Chang-Fang is confused
because his relatives are all mega old for some reason
and he is like "Mom, why are you guys so old?
I was only gone for like a day."
And his mom is like "WRONG, SON.
YOU WERE GONE FOR FIFTEEN YEARS
BECAUSE OF CELESTIAL TIME DILATION."
And Chang-Fang is like "Oh dang.
Well . . . I gotta go help people now
with my magic drugs.
I'll try to visit sometimes."

So then he travels all over the place
healing the sick and capturing demons and stuff
and eventually dies
because he refused to eat poop that one time
although I'm not really sure
whether Chang-Fang really had a chance
or if that whole poop mountain thing was just that
    asshole immortal's idea of a really great prank
which just goes to show
that you should never eat poop
or the maggots that live in poop
no matter who tells you to
or what they are offering.

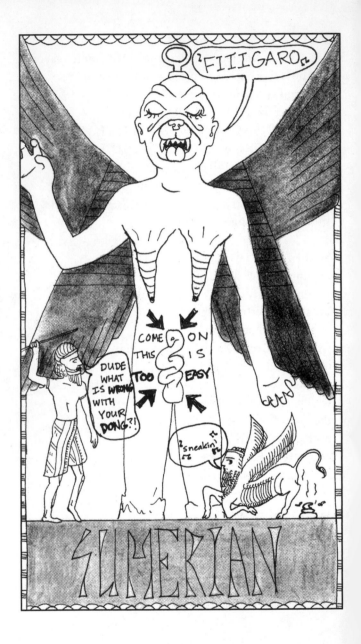

SUMERIAN

A long time ago, there was this place called Sumeria
it was a pretty cool place
or at least, I like to think it was a pretty cool place.
There's not really that much to go on, honestly.
See, people don't actually know that much about
    Sumeria, because of how old it is
and also because apparently these dudes used to party
    so hard
that they seriously damaged a lot of the big clay blocks
    they used to keep their writing on
so the best we can do
is to kind of stare really hard
at the blank spaces on their clay tablets
and make shit up.
For a prime example
check out *Snow Crash* by Neal Stephenson.
For a SUPER-PRIME example
check out this bucket of nonsense.

✦ ✦ ✦

THE ANCIENT SUMERIANS KNEW HOW TO PARTY

So to start out
there is this husband-and-wife god-team.
The dude is named An, and the lady is named Ki.
They make the world, blah blah blah.
When I say "blah blah blah," what I mean is that most
    of the words about that part got destroyed
probably while some lush of a priest was attempting a
    prehistoric kegstand.
What I CAN tell you
is that the water is supposed to have given birth
to all the stuff that's in the world
which makes sense, because water is pretty important
and also because in Sumerian
"water" and "semen" are the SAME WORD
which must have made for some WACKY
    MISUNDERSTANDINGS.

Anyway, once the world has already gotten made and
    stuff
Ki's son Enlil totally steals her
from her husband/his dad
which is GROSS, but definitely not unprecedented
and then I guess all the other gods get the memo that it
    is people-stealin' time
because after another chunk of party-foul-induced
    relic damage

we cut back in to see this chick named Ereshkegal
getting carried down to the underworld.
So this other dude, Enki
the god of water and being a huge nerd all the time
is like "I'll save you, Ereshkegallll!"
So he gets on a boat
which seems like an unnecessary step for a god of
     water
but then his boat sinks
which is DEFINITELY something that should never
     happen to the god of water
but then later Ereshkegal becomes queen of the
     underworld
so it all works out pretty well for her.

But that's not all
because we have yet to address the most well-
     preserved part of this tale of fail:
HOW THE MOON GOT MADE.
See, there's this chick Ninlil
(who is the goddess of wind)
and her mom, Ninshebargunu, is like "Daughter
I want you to promise me
that you will not go swimming in the canal.
If you do, Enlil will see you, and he will totally sex
     you up.
You know how gods are."
So obviously Ninlil nearly breaks her neck trying to
     get down to the canal
and then five minutes later, Enlil shows up
all like "HEY, PRETTY GIRL
I JUST INVENTED THIS NEW GAME
IT IS CALLED JUST THE TIP.
WOULD YOU LIKE TO PLAY?"
And Ninlil is like "Ew, dude. I'm like twelve."

And Enlil is like "Wait, I thought your mom told you
    how this was gonna go down.
Oh well."
Then he rapes her in a boat.

So Ninlil gets pregnant
and everyone gets understandably pissed off at Enlil
and they actually manage to get him banned from
    town as a registered sex offender
so he leaves
and Ninlil follows him
presumably because Enlil conveniently forgot
to make any arrangements regarding child support.
But it turns out that following Enlil
is a really bad idea
because he is so bummed out by this turn of events
that he has decided to walk STRAIGHT TO HELL
and there is some weird rule that says that if your baby
    gets born in hell it has to stay there.
Now, Enlil knows about this rule
and he feels pretty bad about it
so he concocts this genius plan:

When Ninlil arrives at the gates of the underworld
there is a dude in a guard costume with a nametag that
    says "DEFINITELY NOT ENLIL"
and the guard is like "Hey, girl
I see you want to get into hell.
Unfortunately, there is a cover charge
and the cover charge is having sex with me."
So Ninlil is just like "Uh . . . Okay!"
And then they bang
and she gets DOUBLE-PREGNANT.
Then she goes to the next gate into hell
and Enlil pulls the same prank AGAIN.
Then he does it A THIRD TIME.

Now, it may seem like Enlil is just trying to get his
    bone on with the same chick in several costumes
but while that is definitely PART of his motivation
this whole zany sexcapade has the effect of filling
    Ninlil's womb with expendable children
who will stay in hell instead of the first baby
who is named Nanna
and is destined to be the MOON.
So that's where the moon comes from.

So the moral of the story
is that any problem caused by sex
can be easily solved by MORE SEX.

◆ ◆ ◆

Enki and Nimmah Party
Far Too Heartily

So when last we left our Sumerian gods
they were all busy stealing each other and crashing
    boats and prank-sexing each other in costumes.
But in the interim
things seem to have slowed down a bit.
Now all the gods are working in the fields
for minimum wage
just so that they can get something to EAT.
Wait, what?
These are the gods we are talking about
the asshole children with superpowers who run the
    universe

and here they are, SHARECROPPING?
What gives?

Well, that's exactly what all the gods are saying to
    themselves
when suddenly, it hits them:
This kind of boring shit is what PEOPLE are for
And they TOTALLY FORGOT TO INVENT
    THOSE.
So they get some clay
and they mold it into some dude shapes
and then they stick it in a mother goddess for a while
and BOOM
PEOPLE!
So now the gods have someone to do all the farmwork
    for them
and they can get back
to the preferred Sumerian pastime:
PARTYING.

Everybody gets pretty wasted
especially Enki
and this womb goddess named Nimmah.
So they're hitting on each other
in the way only drunk people can:
Nimmah is like "DUDE
    YOU ARE SO WORTHLESS.
WITHOUT MY SICK WOMB SKILLS
ALL THE DUDES WOULD BE DEFORMED."
And Enki is like "PISH POSH, MY FRIEND.
YOU CAN MAKE DUDES AS DEFORMED AS
    YOU PLEASE
AND I CAN STILL FIND JOBS FOR THEM."
So obviously this turns into a contest.
Nimmah goes about trying to invent the most
    messed-up dudes she can

and Enki is passing out jobs like a prostitute on a hot
    streak.
It's like
Parkinson's?
GRAND VIZIER.
No dick?
ROYAL GUARD.
No eyes?
WOMAN, HAVE YOU EVER HEARD OF A DUDE
    BY THE NAME OF HOMER?

So this goes on for a while
and finally Nimmah is like "Ugh, fine.
I guess god CAN'T make a dude so messed up
that even he can't employ him."
And Enki is like "Not so fast, sugarpants. Let me try."
And he picks up the clay
and he just makes the most utterly hideous sack of
    meat and pain
ever to grace the flesh circus.
This thing's spine is all crooked
and its hands are shaking
and its butthole is all caved in
and it can't walk without its feet busting open.
Nimmah tries to feed it some bread
but it can't even EAT.
And Nimmah is like "Whoa, dude, what's your secret?"
And Enki is like "Oh, I just didn't put it in a womb
'cause I don't have one.
This baby is PREMATURE."
And Nimmah's like "Oh . . .
Oh god.
It is just now dawning on me
how completely gross this all is.
Let's try to never do this again, okay?"
But joke's on them, because that stuff still happens.

Except that
as is usually the case when the joke is on the gods
the joke is actually on us.

So the moral of the story
is that you should never get drunk when you have
    superpowers.

❖ ❖ ❖

Gilgamesh and Enkidu: ULTIMATE BROMANCE

Oh my gods and goddesses.
Have you heard about this Gilgamesh guy?
Seriously, the ancient Sumerians actually describe him
as a dude who is "perfect in awesomeness."
Also, his dad is some random dude but his mom is a
    goddess who bangs his dad SO HARD
that Gilgamesh is TWO-THIRDS GOD
AND ONE-THIRD HUMAN
THAT'S RIGHT
they bone with SUCH FURIOUS DEDICATION
that they DESTROY MATH.

But here is the problem, guys:
Gilgamesh is such a badass
he cannot comprehend how people can be ANY LESS
    BADASS THAN HE
so he makes all the dudes in the city he is king of
constantly do feats of strength with him

and also there is a law
that Gilgamesh gets to bone everyone's wives.
So everyone's bitching to the goddess Eiru
like "Hey, Eiru
can you make a dude who is a bad enough dude to
    cockwrestle Gilgamesh?
Because we are worried that if you do not
Gilgamesh will sex us all to death."
And Eiru is like "WELL
I was wondering what to do with this rock I have.
BOOM. NOW IT IS A PERSON."

This guy that Eiru creates is called Enkidu
and he is basically just Cousin Itt from *The Addams
    Family*
if Cousin Itt had the ability to TEAR YOU IN HALF
AND THEN FEED YOU TO YOURSELF.
He pretty much just runs screaming through the forest
punching bears, every day
until one day some namby-pamby hunter sees him
drinking water with all his sweet animal pals
and the hunter is like "THAT DUDE IS SO MANLY
HE MADE MY GUN GO LIMP"
And he goes and asks someone else to help him get rid
    of this hairy dude
but the dude he is whining to is like "Dude, chill OUT.
Just go hit up Gilgamesh for one of his many, many
    whores
and then get Enkidu to bang that whore
and then all his animal magnetism
will get sucked into the whore.
BOOM. SCIENCE."

So the hunter goes to Gilgamesh, who hooks him up
with an exceedingly legitimate ho
and he brings her back to the ol' watering hole

and she flashes her tits at Enkidu
and then they proceed to bang
for SEVEN DAYS STRAIGHT
and afterward the ho makes Enkidu take a shower
which scares away all his animal pals
because animals do not like hygiene.
So Enkidu is like "Damn, I gots to find me the source
 of all these comely hos."
so he goes back to Gilgamesh's kingdom
where Gilgamesh is right in the middle of trying to
 bang some dude's wife
and Enkidu shows up like "Dude
what the hell are you doing?
WANNA BEAT THE SHIT OUT OF EACH
 OTHER INSTEAD?"
And Gilgamesh is like "YESSSS."
so they punch at each other
until they get tired of gargling their own teeth
and then decide to be BFFs.
I am not a scientist, but this may be why women live
 longer than men.

Anyway, their first act as ULTIMATE BESTIES
is to walk all the way across the known world
to punch Humbaba, the magic tree guardian.
Humbaba is not a bad dude or anything
he's really more like those hippies
 that chain themselves to live oaks and whatnot
except he has INTESTINES all over his face
and his breath
is a combination of DEATH and FIRE.
Anyway, Gilgamesh and Enkidu skip off toward this
 sacred cedar tree
LITERALLY HOLDING HANDS.
IT IS ADORABLE.

They skip for LEAGUES AND LEAGUES AND
　　LEAGUES
and Gilgamesh keeps waking up in the middle of the
　　night like "BRO, I HAD A BAD DREAM
IT WAS ABOUT VOLCANOS OR FIRE-
　　BREATHING BIRDS OR LIGHTNING OR
　　SOMETHING."
And Enkidu is like "Naw, bro, those are totally sweet
　　and appropriate things to dream about."
BUT THEN THEY FINALLY FIND HUMBABA'S
　　FOREST
and Humbaba pops out like "'Sup."
And then this god Shamash
who is apparently the sun god
suddenly shows up and hits Humbaba with ALL THE
　　WINDS.
First there's the winds you would expect
like north, south, east, etc.
Then there's some kinda reasonable stuff
like blizzard, storm, and sandstorm.
But then shit really flies off the handle
and we get whistling wind, ice wind, demon wind
and just straight up BAD WIND.
Anyway, all those winds immobilize Humbaba
in an aethereal *bukkake* throwdown
so Gilgamesh is about to chop off Humbaba's head
and Humbaba is like "DUDE
WE ARE IN A FOREST.
THERE IS WOOD LITERALLY COMING OUT
　　OF OTHER WOOD.
YOU DO NOT NEED TO MURDER ME FOR
　　THIS SPECIFIC TREE."
But Gilgamesh murders him anyway
and then he's like "Sweet
now I can use this tree to make a huge door.

I don't really have a place to put a huge door right now
but like my grand-pappy used to say:
'You never know when you're gonna need a really huge
    door.' "

So they're back at home, enjoying this sweet door
and also each other's company
when Ishtar has to come along and fuck it all up.
(Ishtar, by the way
is the goddess of basically everything worth doing:
sex, war, and babies.
Wait, I don't mean that you should do babies, though.
That is gross/illegal.)
So Ishtar is like "HEY, GILGAMESH
I HAVE THIS GAPING HOLE IN MY BODY
I'M WORRIED IT MIGHT JUST START
    SHOOTING OUT MY ORGANS OR
    SOMETHING
I HEAR YOU HAVE SOMETHING ABOUT THE
    RIGHT SIZE TO PLUG THIS HOLE
IF YOU KNOW WHAT I MEAN."
And Gilgamesh is like "Whoa, girl, slow your roll.
Your tits are exceedingly fine
but I am aware of a little something called history
and history tells us that every dude you have banged
has either caught on fire or turned into a dwarf.
I am sure there are dongs aplenty in this kingdom
    of mine.
Go nuts.
Just steer clear of MY nuts."
So Ishtar goes up to Godtowne and she is like "GUYS
GILGAMESH WON'T STUFF MY MUFF.
GIVE ME THE BULL OF HEAVEN SO I CAN GO
    RUIN EVERYTHING."
Yeah, apparently they keep this bull around
for if they ever need to ruin everything

and the gods are pretty laissez-faire
about how it gets used
so Ishtar drags the bull down to earth
and Gilgamesh eventually sees it
after it's killed like a million people
and then he and Enkidu are like "BEST BUDS TAG-
    TEAM MURDERCYCLE YEAH!"
and they handle the bull to pieces
in a matter of seconds, and steal its horns
and then they high-five so hard
that another thousand or so people die.

BUT ALL IS NOT WELL, MY FRIENDS
because tonight it is ENKIDU'S TURN TO HAVE
    THE DREAMS.
He dreams that the gods are all sitting around
    talking
and they're like "Man,
Enkidu and Gilgamesh are a two-man meatgrinder
grindin' up all our best abominations.
We gotta kill one of them, but we can't kill Gilgamesh
his name is in the title.
Guess we better kill Enkidu, huh?"
And Enkidu wakes up like "THERE IS NO
    POSSIBLE WAY TO INTERPRET THIS
    FAVORABLY."
Then he gets real sick and he dies.

Now, we all know about the nine stages of grief or
    whatever
but those are for CHUMPS.
Gilgamesh's grieving process has three steps:
Step one: Cry about it.
Step two: Make everyone else cry about it
using your fists.
Step three: SEEK IMMORTALITY.

So he goes and talks smack to some scorpion dudes,
who let him walk through a mountain
and then on the other side he finds
THE WATERS OF DEATH
which is probably not the first place I would look
if I were searching for immortality
but anyway, there is an inn there
and Gilgamesh threatens the innkeeper
until she tells him how to get across the water
and then he threatens the guy who can get him across
    the water
and then he has to rebuild the boat he destroyed while
    threatening that guy
but finally they sail to the other side
which is where Gilgamesh was trying to get, apparently.
And there's this dude there called Utnapishtim
and he's like "Whoa, you got some balls coming over
    here, son. What's your name?"
and Gilgamesh is like "I'M GILGAMESH.
MY BEST PAL DIED
NOW I WANNA BE IMMORTAL."
And Utnapishtim is like "That is the most weak-sauce
    reason anyone has given me to do anything.
But anyway, let me tell you my life story:"
SUMMARY:
UTNAPISHTIM IS NOAH
EXCEPT HE SAVES A LOT MORE HUMANS
AND THEN HE GETS TO BE IMMORTAL
THE END.
And after his story, Utnapishtim is like "So, you see
I busted my ass for immortality
and frankly
I don't think the gods are down to do that again.
You may want to just take your punk ass back across
    the waters of death and go die like a man."
But joke's on Utnapishtim

because Gilgamesh got so bored of the story
that he actually FELL ASLEEP.
But actually, joke's on Gilgamesh
because Utnapishtim bakes a ton of bread
and puts it next to Gilgamesh's face
so that when he wakes up SEVEN DAYS LATER
he sees all this moldy bread and he is like "Ew, gross."
But then I guess Utnapishtim feels bad about his prank
so he tells Gilgamesh about this weird immortality
       plant that grows at the bottom of the ocean
and then obviously Gilgamesh ties rocks to his feet
and sinks to the bottom of the ocean
(Again, this does not seem like the behavior
of a dude who is trying to not die)
and he gets this plant
but then he stops to take a bath on his way back home
and a snake steals the plant
and then eventually Gilgamesh gets old and dies
miserable and alone
or maybe content and surrounded by whores.
The epic is not clear on this point.

So basically
Enkidu wouldn't have died if that chick hadn't boned
       him and then made him take a shower
and Gilgamesh would've had eternal youth if he hadn't
       stopped for a bath
so the moral of the story
is that REAL HEROES NEVER BATHE.

NATIVE AMERICAN

Now the problem with dedicating a section
to the whole of Native American mythology
is that there were a lot of people living in this country
before we showed up and set it on fire
and some of them didn't get along too well
and they ALL had their own stories
so trying to tell a cohesive Native American
    mythology
with only a handful of myths
is a lot like trying to cook an alphabet soup using only
    the letter "A"
so I highly recommend that you go online
and look up some Native American myths on
    your own
because there's a TON of them
and they're great
but for now
I am going to attempt to give you a small spoonful
of the alphabet soup that this country used to belong to.

WISAKEDJAK IS HIGHLY IRRESPONSIBLE

Now I know I told you there were a thousand and one
    pantheons to choose from here
but at least as far as creation myths are concerned
all the Native American stories start to sound pretty
    much the same after a while
so I picked the Algonquin version
because it is the one with the highest concentration of
    hilarious jerks.

Speaking of hilarious jerks, meet Wisakedjak.
His name is sometimes anglicized as Whiskey Jack
but that's needlessly confusing
'cause this dude has nothing to do with whiskey
and in fact was around WAYYYY before whiskey
because what kind of creation myth would this be
    otherwise?
A much drunker one, that's what kind.

But Wisakedjak is not the kind of dude who NEEDS
    whiskey to get down.
See, he's a trickster god
who happens to be real tight with the creator.
So basically
the creator makes the world
and then he's like "Dude, Wisakedjak
I am so tired from making this world and stuff.
How about you handle everything else now.

Like, teach everyone what roots are good to eat
and keep them from killing each other and stuff.
You know, pretty much everything I am actually
     personally responsible for doing
but like, the not-fun part of it."
So the creator goes to sleep
and Wisakedjak proceeds to do the exact opposite
of everything the creator told him to do
as in, he feeds everyone poison
and goes around starting fights.
So then the creator wakes up from like a ten-year nap
and he's like "Whooooaaaa, dude.
What did I tell you to do?
I'm pretty sure it wasn't that.
You best clean up your act
Or else I'm gonna kill everybody
and then you'll be bored."
So Wisakedjak calls bullshit
and just goes right on doing what he was doing
except like NINE TIMES HARDERRRR
he is running up to dudes like "HEY:
HEYYYY:
SEE THAT GUY OVER THERE?
HE KILLED YOUR DOG
HE KILLED YOUR PARENTS
MURDER HIM.
EAT THIS CYANIDE.
GO GO GO."
And he just keeps doing this
until the earth is literally saturated with blood
there is nowhere for all this blood to go
it's pretty upsetting
so at this point the creator shows up again
like "THAT'S IT.
EVERYBODY DIES."
So then everything floods, as usual

and the only things left alive
are Wisakedjak
(even though he is almost the entire problem)
plus an otter, a beaver, and a muskrat.
No fish, apparently
which is something I always wonder about in these
    flood myths.
Like, a flood seems like a really great way
to punish every living creature in the world
except for fish.
What the hell is a god supposed to do
when all the FISH start being assholes?

Anyway, let's just sidestep that plothole completely
and cut to Wisakedjak sitting in the water with his
    animal pals
crying and feeling sorry for himself
when all of a sudden he has an idea.
He's like "DUDES:
I can't create anything
'cause I spent all my attribute points on being a dick
but I CAN infinitely expand anything that has already
    been created.
So I need one of you guys to dive all the way to the
    bottom of this water
and get me some dirt to expand.
HEY, CREATOR
IT'S OKAY IF I DO THIS, RIGHT?"
And the creator is like "Sure
you can make a new world
as long as you use all the material I wasted on the old
    world.
I don't wanna have to go out and get a bunch of new
    dirt and whatnot."
Man
the Algonquin people have them one LAZY creator.

So Wisakedjak is like "OTTER
YOU'RE SO BRAVE
GO DO IT AND I'LL MAKE SURE YOU ALWAYS
     HAVE FISH TO EAT"
so otter dives down
and comes back up with NO DIRT AT ALL
and he keeps trying
until he is too weak to dive anymore
and Wisakedjak is like "Wow, dude
I am pretty disappointed in you.
Okay, it's beaver's turn.
Beaver, if you bring me some dirt
then I will build you a house"
so beaver dives
and I'm pretty sure we all know how that turns out
because it's not like beavers live in five-star hotels
is it?
So finally Wisakedjak turns to the muskrat
and he's like "All right, my man
I do not have high hopes for you.
In fact my hopes for you are practically subterranean.
But that may actually work in our favor in this
     situation
so if you make it to the bottom
I'll give you infinite roots to eat forever
plus rushes to make a house out of
and you'll have, like, a billion babies. Seriously."
So muskrat dives
and he comes up
and he has
NO DIRT
so he tries again
and he's gone for a while
and he comes up real tired
and he still has no dirt
but here's the important thing:

He SMELLS like dirt.
So Wisakedjak is like "Dude, you are so close.
Try one more time."
So the muskrat dives down
and he's gone for a LOOOONG time
and everyone is pretty sure he's dead.
But then they see some bubbles
so they reach in and pull out the muskrat
who is pretty much dead
but he has just a little bit of dirt with him
which Wisakedjak turns into an island
and then they finally get to stop sitting in the water.

So then in the following days
Wisakedjak finds some bones
and uses them to make animals
and he makes trees out of some wood
and then the creator waits for him to finish all this
    work
and then he's like "All right, dude.
I just decided you don't get to have powers anymore.
You just get the power to lie like a motherfucker."
So Wisakedjak just uses that power as hard as he can
for ever and ever
starting by failing to ever reward the muskrat
because at the end of the day
what worse punishment is there
than being a muskrat?

So the moral of the story
is practice holding your breath
it's good for more than just weird sex stuff.

♦ ♦ ♦

KILLER-OF-ENEMIES AND THE INTERNATIONAL HOUSE OF VAGINAS

So this is one of those myths
where I almost don't even need to retell it
I could just transcribe it word for word
and it would just end up looking like something I
    made up.
Watch:

So there's this house full of vaginas, right?
Yup.
Just a big ol' house stuffed full of vaginas.
They have actually got vaginas hanging on the walls
thick as wall scrolls in an *otaku*'s cave.
My friends, this is the quintessential tunaparty
tacofest
clambake
cervical circus
this place is lousy with vaginas, is what I'm saying.

But the lousiest vaginas of all
are these four girls called the vagina girls.
They are actually just giant vaginas.
Giant, shape-shifting vaginas that look like girls.
Oh, also
there are no vaginas anywhere else on earth at this point.
This place is essentially the Fort Knox of vagina

except the security team is actually just one guy
or actually one monster, named Kicking Monster
whose MO is to roll up on any poor jerk who enters
    the vicinity
and kick him INTO THE HOUSE.
This is not how guards work usually
but hey
no one who gets kicked into the house ever leaves
so Kicking Monster must be doing something right
although I think that may have more to do with the fact
that this is a house
filled with ALL OF THE VAGINAS.

But even despite Kicking Monster
dudes are lining up around the block to take a crack at
    this vagina house
because let me reiterate
this is a house full of ALL THE VAGINAS
That would be like if someone took all the
well
it would be like if someone took all the vaginas in the
    world and put them in one house.
I don't know how to make it any clearer than that.

So dudes keep mysteriously disappearing into this
    vagina house
until finally this one badass rolls up
named Killer-of-Enemies
Who is much more popular than his little brother
Killer-of-Babies-and-Small-Woodland-Creatures
and Killer-of-Enemies takes it upon himself
to fix this vagina problem.
So he kicks Kicking Monster in the nuts and he busts
    into the house
and here come the four beautiful vagina girls
like "OH MY GOD, TAKE US NOW."

And Killer-of-Enemies is like
"That is a tempting offer
but first I gotta ask you ladies
what happened to all the dudes who got kicked in
    here?"
And the vagina girls are like "Oh
we ate them with our vaginas
which are also our whole bodies
and are full of thousands of incredibly sharp teeth
like in a horror movie.
That's kinda what we do."
And Killer-of-Enemies is like "WHAT?
THAT'S NOT HOW YOU USE A VAGINA.
Look, ladies
I'm totally down for some frisky sexin'
but first you gotta take these drugs I brought with me."
And the vagina girls are like "FREE DRUGS?
COUNT US IN."
So Killer-of-Enemies feeds these girls sour berries
which are actually just a ton of Rohypnol and ecstasy
and also some kind of tooth-decaying powder
to remove their unpleasant vag teeth
and the vagina girls are like "OH MY GOD
THIS SEX FEELS SO GOOD."
And Killer-of-Enemies is like "Dang, girls
I ain't even banged you yet."
And then later he totally bangs them
right in their domesticated vaginas
and I guess he probably distributes the loose assorted
    vaginas amongst the people
and no one has to deal with unsightly vagina teeth or
    women's rights ever again.

So the moral of the story
is that people who live in vagina houses
should not get stoned.

◆ ◆ ◆

Rabbit Takes Summer Fun to the Next Level

Summer can be a drag
but what if you could solve summer
using VIOLENCE?
Well, my friends, it turns out you can
as long as you are a mythical rabbit
with unlimited reserves of CHUTZPAH.

See, once upon a time the sun used to be even more of
    a bastard than it is now.
It would take a flying leap off the horizon in the
    morning
and then spend the rest of the day
doing flaming kickflips of disaster off the clouds.
But one day
Rabbit decides he has had enough of this nonsense.
He is trying to get his chill on
in the shade of a shady oak tree
but the sun is just pretty much PRYING THE
    SHADOWS STRAIGHT OFF HIM
and then BAKING CANCER INTO HIS SKIN.
Anyway, Rabbit is not about to take guff
from some puffed-up ball of superheated gases
so he grabs his gun
and he starts walking.

Yes, of course I can repeat that:
Rabbit grabs a GUN

and he starts walking east, to where the sun lives
so that he can SHOOT THE SUN FOR BEING
    TOO HOT.

So Rabbit is stomping his way to the horizon
and on the way, he *practices*
which yes, means exactly what you think it means.
It means this rabbit is stomping his way to the horizon
shooting *EVERYTHING*.
Rocks
lizards
other rabbits.
Nothing can escape Rabbit's sociopathic target
    practice.
But finally he gets to the horizon
and this is before sunrise, you understand
so he's sitting there waiting for the sun to come up.
But the problem with crossing an entire world
while firing your gun constantly
is that it tends to sort of telegraph your future plans
so the sun already knows what's up
and it responds by rising REALLY FAST
and off to one side
which totally fakes Rabbit out
and by the time he gets a bead on the sun
it is already too far away to shoot.

But Rabbit is not gonna give up that easily.
This is a dude who is SERIOUS about taking naps
    under trees.
So he sits there for DAYS
while the sun continues to fake his ass out.
Sometimes it rises to the left
sometimes to the right
sometimes it does barrel rolls and cartwheels

and all this time, Rabbit stays right there
WAITING for the sun to fuck up.

It is terrifying to me to imagine
that the sun is capable of EVER making mistakes
but that is exactly what it does.
Maybe it comes up a little too slow
or in the wrong place
but whatever it is, Rabbit is ready for it
and he shoots it RIGHT IN THE FACE.
So hooray, right? The sun is wounded
and we have all learned a valuable lesson.
NOT SO FAST.
See, the thing about the sun—
and you would think that Rabbit might have
    considered this—
is that it is a giant ball of superheated hatred
that BLEEDS FIRE.
So while Rabbit is busy congratulating himself on his
    expert marksmanship
the sun is busy bleeding a geyser of piping hot
    apocalypse all over the world.
Now, Rabbit is not about to pull off the greatest
    drive-by in history
just to get barbecued by a celestial body
so he starts running for cover
and the first cover he finds is a big tree
so he comes running up to the tree, like "Quick! Tree!
Hide me under your branches!"
And the tree is like "Dude, I am a *tree*.
I am made of *wood*.
Have you considered hiding under *non*flammable
    things?"
So Rabbit keeps running, asking all the trees to
    shelter him

and they keep saying no, because they are *trees*.
But finally, Rabbit manages to con this bush into
    sheltering him
and then the sun's fire passes over them
and all that happens to the bush is that the leaves turn
    kind of yellow forever
which isn't that bad, all things considered.

But there *are* real consequences to this cavalcade of
    tomfoolery.
For one thing, Rabbit is afflicted with a serious case
    of PTSD
which is why rabbits are total wusses nowadays.
The sun survives the ordeal somehow
But it's hard to do your job
when you're worried someone is gonna shoot you
every time you clock in
which is why the sun rises really slowly and
    cautiously now
and also why it is so bright:
It is so that you cannot get a good bead on it with a
    sniper rifle.

So the moral of the story
is that we don't need to worry about global warming
as long as we have guns.

The end.

♦ ♦ ♦

THE MOON IS
MADE OF MEAT

So there's this place in Idaho or Montana or
    something, and it has no moon.
Everyone hates it , because how are they supposed to
    have sexy late-night disco parties?
Electricity has not been invented yet, my friends.
This is what was once known as BAD TIMES FOR
    DISCO.

So everyone gets together and they're like "Guys
we need a MOON.
Then we can truly boogie
ALL NIGHT LONG
without someone tripping and putting his face through
    a disco ball like LAST TIME.
I mean, whose bright idea was it to bring a disco ball
to a party WITHOUT ANY LIGHTS?
But okay, let's see . . .
What do we have a lot of that we're not using?
Oh, that's right.
ANIMALS."

So they call up all the animals, and they are like "Okay
here's how it's gonna be:
One of you is going to crawl up into the sky
and curl up into a ball
and reflect sunlight at us while we boogie
ALL NIGHT LONG."

And Fox
who is dumb and eager to please
is like "OH MAN, GUYS
I WILL BE THE BEST MOON."
So he runs up into the sky
and he curls himself up into a ball
and he starts reflecting the PANTS off that sun
which is quite an achievement
because I didn't know the sun wore pants.
But here's the problem, my friends:
Fox is WAY TOO GOOD AT HIS JOB.
It's like straight-up daylight all over the place.
Everyone caught with their wangs out on the dance
    floor
totally embarrassed.
So everybody's like "Sorry, Fox
but we need a little more mood lighting for this sexy
    party we're having.
Gonna need you to step down from the sky."
And Fox is like "Aww, okay."
And then Raven is like "OH SNAP
NOW'S MY CHANCE.
NOTHING IS SEXIER THAN BLACKLIGHT."
So raven flies up there and balls himself up
but as everybody but Raven already knows
black is TERRIBLE for reflecting sunlight
so pretty soon everyone is right back to putting various
    parts of their anatomy through disco balls.
DID YOU KNOW: Disco balls are not actually in this
    story and I am just making that part up.

Anyway, everybody gets their shit straightened out
and cleans all the blood off their faces and wangs
and then they're like "Okay, Raven
I know we said we wanted someone to be less good at
    their job

but we did not mean for someone to come in and drive
    the failbus straight off a cliff."
So Raven slinks back down to earth, all humiliated
because at least Fox only got fired for being too GOOD
    at his job
and it is at this point that Coyote decides to make his
    move.
He shows up like "GUYS, LOOK AT ME.
MY FUR IS EXACTLY THE RIGHT COLOR.
THIS IS ONE JOB SITUATION
WHERE RACIAL PROFILING
IS TOTALLY OKAY."
And everyone is like "Well, we are uncomfortable with
    your rhetoric, but okay."

So Coyote gets his ass up in the sky
and curls into a ball
and it's perfect, it's great.
Everyone is dancing up a storm
but not a literal storm.
(That would be bad
and probably interrupt the dancing.)
No, this is a figurative storm
composed of gyrating pelvii and windmilling dangly
    bits.
It's great. You would have loved it.
But then Coyote gets all bored
'cause this dude has some serious ADD
so he starts using his privileged position up in the sky
to get all up in everyone's business.
He's all peeping in the ladies' windows
like "HEY, EVERYONE
SUSAN JUST INVENTED THE STAR-GROPE.
COME LOOK."
And everyone comes and looks
except for Susan, who doesn't come at all

because a screaming busybody moon
is the ultimate mood killer.
Coyote also uses his moon powers to keep homeless
    guys from stealing food and to cheat at cards.
So everyone gets pissed off, and they decide to fire him.

But he's like "HAHA, YOU CAN'T REALLY FIRE ME.
I'M THE PERFECT COLOR."
and everyone is like "Dude
there are pretty much a hojillion animals
with the same color fur as you.
Case in point: Rabbit
and Rabbit is not such a fucking spaz either."
so they send Rabbit up to be the moon
and Rabbit ends up being pretty chill about the whole
    thing
FOREVER.
And that is why Coyote is always howling at the moon.
It's because he just cannot get over that stuff that
    happened that one time.

So the moral of the story
is that we should seriously consider firing the moon
because I didn't know we could do that
and I bet we have the technology now
to genetically engineer a WAY BETTER MOON
than some dumb rabbit.

UNITED STATES
OF AMERICAN

So first, a quick disclaimer:
Throughout this section, I'm gonna be calling the
    United States of America "AMERICA"
and you are going to deal with this
because America is just flat out easier to type than
    "The States"
or "The U.S. of A."
or "That Big Basket of Jerks under Canada"
But second off, don't you think it's weird
that of all the myriad ethnic groups we have
    shoehorned together in this wide western world
    of ours
our predominant mythological tradition
is tied to a bunch of ancient dead dudes
whose religion no one even worships anymore?
Now, I'm not denying Greek myths are super sweet
there is nothing better, if you want to watch a bunch of
    children boinking and killing each other.
But I feel like it is my duty as an American
to raise awareness
of some goddamn AMERICAN MYTHOLOGY UP
    IN HERE.
But there's a problem:
America is not very old, my friends.
We have not had time to develop a really spectacular
    cast of magical jerks to talk about.
Oh snap, wait a second.

I totally take that back.
We've got a whole pantheon of crazy dudes to
      choose from
and they are called
THE FOUNDING FATHERS
but I could write a whole other book about those guys
and maybe someday I will
so for now, you're gonna have to settle
for a whirlwind tour
OF THE MYTHOLOGY WE'VE MADE SO FAR.

◆ ◆ ◆

THE CREATION MYTH . . .
OF AMERICA

Now, normally in these creation myths
we start out with a vast ocean
and then some guy comes along and puts land in it.
America is no exception.
This time, the ocean is called the Atlantic Ocean
and the guy is called Christopher Columbus.
The only difference
is that Columbus doesn't MAKE the land
he just finds it, on his way to go find something else
because apparently some gods put it there a long time
        ago and forgot to tell anyone about it.
There are also already people in this America place
but that's not a big deal
because people are pretty easy to get rid of.
See also: the biblical flood.
Anyway, for the time being
Christopher Columbus names these people Indians
because that is the name of the people in the place he
        was supposed to be looking for
and he is still laboring under some misapprehensions.

Time passes
and a bunch of Christopher Columbus's friends
        show up
a whole pantheon of legendary bastards called the
        conquistadors
and they populate the land with themselves

while depopulating the land of everybody else.
Then even MORE time passes
and some other guys start showing up
from this place called the BRITISH EMPIRE
which sounds like it must be a pretty nice place.
Like, the sun never sets there
so it's basically an eternal beach party all the time
but with more fog.
But even so
tons of dudes keep getting on boats and leaving
and sailing across a WHOLE OCEAN
to get to this hip new America place everyone is
      talking about
because Britain is nice and everything
but it is totally played out.

Amongst the British dudes who show up
are a bunch of people who are practicing this crazy
      souped-up version of Christianity.
In this scenario, they will be our CHOSEN PEOPLE.
They meet all the requirements:
(1) They are the dudes who ultimately get the
      promised land
and (2) They get the promised land by killing a
      WHOLE BUNCH OF PEOPLE.
Yeah, basically what happens
is that they're hanging out in America for a while
when suddenly, the king of England
(who is named George)
starts being a TOTAL DICK.
He's like
"I PUT ALL YOU PEOPLE IN THIS NEW LAND.
NOW YOU HAVE TO PAY TRIBUTE TO ME."
But all the American dudes are like "No way!"
And then instead of killing them with a massive flood
like a REAL divine emperor would have

King George tries to kill them with an army of really
    flashily dressed guys.
But as we have already established
guys are REALLY easy to kill
and they are even easier to kill
when they are covered in bright red dress-coats
so the Americans just get a whole bunch of guns
and shoot at England until it goes away
and then they shoot at the conquistadors
until they go away too.
Then they shoot at the natives
and then when they run out of natives
they shoot at each other.
Then they've still got a lot of bullets left over
so they have to keep finding more people to shoot.
Also, I think someone writes a constitution?
Anyway, that's where America comes from.

So the moral of the story
is that the primary ingredient for a successful nation
is guns.

◆ ◆ ◆

JOHN HENRY WAS A
STEEL-DRIVIN' MAN

I SAID, JOHN HENRY WAS A STEEL-DRIVIN'
    MAN.

Do you guys know what that means?
That means that he was a dude
who worked on a railroad

and his job
was to KILL MOUNTAINS.
Now, the way he did this
was that some poor sonofabitch named Little Bill
would hold a steel drill in place against the rock
while John Henry BEAT ON IT
AS HARD AS HE COULD
WITH A TWENTY-POUND HAMMER
and Bill had to keep turning the drill after every
    strike
and eventually the drill would get dull
so he had to swap it out
for another drill
that someone would hopefully hand to him
at about that time
WITHOUT MISSING A BEAT
and then they would bring the old drill to a blacksmith
so the blacksmith could fix it
and then bring it back to Bill so he could switch it out
AGAIN
and meanwhile John Henry's hammer is just whistling
    right past Bill's junk
or face, or ribs, or wherever he has to hold the drill
in order to make sure the rock is getting brutalized in
    the right direction.
Meanwhile, John Henry has it easy.
All HE has to do
is heft a TWENTY-POUND HAMMER
over and over again
with perfect accuracy
all day
through solid rock
never stopping, never getting tired
under constant threat of rockslides and disfigurement.

So this is this guy's job.

Now John Henry works for a pack of rat bastards
called the C&O Railroad Company.
I know they are rat bastards
because one day John Henry's railroad team
rolls up on this big, big mountain
and the railroad crew is all like "Oh wow, bummer.
Guess we better start going around this mountain,
      huh?"
And aforementioned rat bastards from C&O
are like "NOPE.
GOIN' STRAIGHT THROUGH THE
      MOUNTAIN.
IT IS ONLY LIKE A MILE AND A HALF THICK.
YOU GUYS LIKE HAVING JOBS, RIGHT?
SO *DO IT*."

So they do it
most of these guys are freed slaves
so they don't exactly have their pick of the crop
as far as employment opportunities go.
This goes double for John Henry
who is not only a freed slave
but also an UNSTOPPABLE BADASS WHO NEVER
      QUITS.
So every day all the steel drivers go to work
and they fling themselves mercilessly at this
      mountain
and like twenty people die
but John Henry just keeps abusing that stone
making a solid ten-foot tunnel every day, at LEAST.
So, you know, great for him
but all his friends are still dead
and the dicks at C&O are getting impatient
so when this traveling salesman shows up
with a steam-powered drill machine
they are like "SIGN US UP.

P.S.: Everyone who works for us is fired now.
ESPECIALLY JOHN HENRY."

Now John Henry is the kind of man
who takes absolutely no guff from anybody.
It is unreal how little guff this man takes.
Like, if there were a great big pile of guff by the side of
    the road
and John Henry walked by
that pile would remain completely undisturbed
because he would take none of it.
So when he sees this guff coming his way
he just sidesteps the lot of it
and then he turns around like "Hey, traveling salesman
I bet I can drill harder, better, faster, AND stronger
than your candyassed machine."
And the traveling salesman is like "YOU'RE ON."
So the next day
John Henry lines up next to this machine
along with his trusty shaker Little Bill
and TWO twenty-pound hammers
and they get. to. work.

So John and the drill are staying pretty much neck
    and neck
even though the drill doesn't have a neck.
Maybe the drill is even doing a little better
but then it gets STUCK in a hole in the rock
and John Henry just goes grunting and flailing and
    sweating
FOURTEEN FEET INTO THE HEART OF THAT
    MOUNTAIN.
BAM CLINK CACHANG POW BOOM PEW PEW
    PEW.
I DON'T KNOW WHAT SOUND A HAMMER
    MAKES.

So, final score:
Newfangled steam drill: nine feet.
One man armed with nothing but sweat and hammers:
fourteen feet.
Oh wait.
Did I forget to mention
that since John Henry is using two hammers, he
        drilled TWO HOLES
while the steam drill only made ONE??
So really, the score was nine to TWENTY-EIGHT.
Yeah.
But there's some bad news too.
See, as soon as he finds out his score
John Henry puts down his hammers and dies
because he just hammered that rock so hard
he gave himself a stroke.
It doesn't say in the ballad
but I like to think that his last words
were something like
". . . Damn right."

Anyway, then he's dead
so I think they end up using the steam drill anyway
although they have to cancel work for like a week
because everyone is convinced
that John Henry's ghost lives in the tunnel
also later on it turns out that the tunnel is notoriously
        unstable
because it is a bad idea to use contests
to construct structurally delicate railway tunnels.

But none of that matters
because the real hero of this story
is Little Bill
who held two drills
right next to all the tenderest parts of his body

against a solid stone wall
while an absurdly muscular dude
repeatedly charged toward him
flailing two twenty-pound hammers.
And he kept holding those drills
and turning them
and shaking out the stone debris
and switching out the drills when they got dull
FOR THIRTY-FIVE MINUTES
AND TWENTY-EIGHT FEET
and he *didn't* have a stroke
or even poop himself a little.

So let's hear it for Little Bill
the real American hero.

◆ ◆ ◆

PAUL BUNYAN WAS A LOG-DRIVIN' MAN

We all know that lumberjacks are badasses.
But have you ever stopped to wonder *how* we know
that?
I'LL TELL YOU HOW.
PAUL BUNYAN IS HOW.
Because that dude
was *big*.
HOW BIG WAS HE?

He was SO BIG
that it took three storks to deliver him to his parents.

He was SO BIG
that when he was old enough to laugh and clap his
    hands
he DESTROYED HIS HOUSE.
He was SO BIG
that one time he dragged his ax behind him when he
    was walking
and made the Grand Canyon.
This guy was BIG.
But all of that is baby stuff, compared with the time he
    tamed the Whistling River.

So the Whistling River
is a river that has somehow come into possession of
    some rudimentary intelligence
and a WHOLE LOT OF GUFF
which it hands out to all comers
because as you may have noticed
guff is America's chief natural resource.
See, this river likes to rear up at random times
    throughout the day
and let out a piercing whistle that annoys the crap out
    of everyone for MILES AROUND.
This river is also a total dick.
It breaks up log rafts
it drowns loggers
it does everything a river is not supposed to do
and laughs about it
or whistles about it, I guess.

But then the river makes a crucial mistake
because one day Paul Bunyan is sitting by the river,
eating some flapjacks
when the river rears up
and chucks FOUR HUNDRED AND NINETEEN
    GALLONS OF MUDDY WATER

INTO HIS BEARD.
Now I'm sure I don't have to tell you
that a lumberjack's beard
is NOT TO BE TRIFLED WITH
but Paul Bunyan gives the river a pass.
He just goes back to his pancakes
and figures the river will behave itself.
But that river rears up
and chucks FIVE THOUSAND AND NINETEEN
    MORE GALLONS
AND SOME TURTLES AND SOME FISH AND
    SOME MUSKRAT
DIRECTLY INTO PAUL BUNYAN'S ALREADY
    SOAKING WET BEARD
plus his flapjacks are pretty wet.
This is the kind of thing any self-respecting lumberjack
    cannot ignore.

So what does Paul Bunyan do?
Does he get up and move someplace where the river
    can't soak him?
NO.
Instead, he decides to TAME the river.
But how?

Well, Paul Bunyan settles down to do some serious
    thinking
and the way lumberjacks think
is they sit down and they eat popcorn
for DAYS.
Paul Bunyan eats so much popcorn
that after a week, the ground is covered with eighteen
    inches of popcorn scraps
for THREE MILES AROUND
and animals that wander into the area immediately
    think it is winter

and freeze to death before they have a chance to
   actually think about what they are doing.

Anyway, finally Paul Bunyan leaps up like "AHA!
I bet if I took all the bends out of the river
it would straighten up and fly right.
So I'll just tie it to Babe, my massive blue ox
and she'll tow it straight.
Oh wait, it's made of water.
How am I going to attach my ox to it?
HMM."

So Paul Bunyan and his ox go to the North Pole
and he makes a box trap baited with icicles
and then goes and plays fetch with Babe for a while
using GLACIERS
but he has to stop because he floods Florida.
Then he goes back to check on his trap
and finds that he has caught SIX BLIZZARDS.
Man, I wish I had a box big enough to catch six
   blizzards.
I'd open up a blizzard stand
and no one would buy any
BECAUSE BLIZZARDS ARE A THING THAT
   NOBODY WANTS.

But Paul Bunyan doesn't see it that way.
He grabs two of those blizzards
and he takes them back to his logging camp
and has his friend Ole—
who is not a lumberjacking matador
but rather a big Swede—
make two huge logging chains to attach to the
   blizzards.
Then he goes to the river and jams the blizzards into it
which freezes it FOR SEVENTEEN MILES

then he hooks the river up to Babe
and it is GO TIME.

But that river is TOOOO ornery
it won't budge
even though Babe pulls those chains into solid iron bars
and digs ruts into the solid rock she is running on.
But that's when Paul Bunyan just cuts straight through
    the bullshit
by grabbing the chains and pulling them so hard
that he and Babe drag the river free of its banks
and through the prairie.
When finally they stop running and turn around
they see that the river has become TOTALLY
    STRAIGHT
but it is also somehow much shorter
because all the elbow joints that made the bends
are now scattered across the prairie.
So Paul Bunyan packs up all the extra bends
and uses them later, when he needs to float logs in the
    middle of the desert
even though that's not how that works
and there aren't even any logs in the desert
because you get to ignore physics
as long as you are really, really big.

Anyway, then the river refuses to whistle
because it has basically just undergone
the river equivalent of traumatic castration
and strangely enough, this makes everyone really
    pissed off at Paul Bunyan
because it turns out that everyone was using the river
    as an alarm clock
and they need to wake up early
because trees are easier to cut down when you catch
    them snoozing.

But luckily this dude comes along
named Squeaky Swanson
who has a speaking voice that is never above a whisper
but a shriek that can physically LIFT THE
    BLANKETS off of everyone in camp.
So every day, Squeaky Swanson wakes up at the crack
    of dawn
and shrieks everyone awake
thus solving every problem forever.

So once again
the real hero of the story is not Paul Bunyan
who actually ruined the whistling river
and broke physics
and littered a lot of popcorn scraps all over
and flooded Florida
but rather an unassuming man
with some kind of weird voice problem.

So God bless America
home of the little guy
as long as the little guy can yell really loud.

❖ ❖ ❖

PECOS BILL WAS A CATTLE-DRIVIN' MAN

All right, my friends.
It is time for you to hear about a man
whose ass is SO BAD
other asses cower at the mere mention of it.

The owner of this ass is named PECOS BILL.

But Pecos Bill was not always named that.
For a while he was just named Bill.
This dude was not alive more than, say, ten seconds
before he started chewing knives and riding horses
and then crawling out of his mom's wagon
when she wasn't looking
and wrestling BEAR CUBS
and WINNING.

But as if that wasn't enough
the way Pecos Bill gets the Pecos part of his name
is that one day his family is crossing the Pecos River
and Bill falls out of the wagon into the water
probably because he was trying to bust out and wrestle
    bears at the wrong time
and his family is like "DAMMIT.
HE WAS GONNA BE SUCH A BADASS."
And then his mom dies of being sad.

But it's okay, guys
because Pecos Bill gets fished out of the river
BY COYOTES.
THAT IS A REASSURING THING TO HAVE
    HAPPEN, RIGHT??
Actually, yes
because in this case, the coyotes make the incredibly
    un-coyote-like decision
to raise this delicious human baby as one of their own
for fifteen years.
Yeah, that's right. He's one of THOSE kids.
But then after fifteen years, Pecos Bill is drinking
from the river that bears his name
when his brother comes along
punching cattle, like people do in Texas.

(I think punching cattle is an expression
meaning to herd cattle or something
but I really prefer to imagine
that Pecos Bill's brother is just SOCKING COWS IN
    THE FOREHEAD
ALL ACROSS THE PRAIRIE.)
Anyway, he sees Pecos Bill squatting by the river
and he's like "HEY
Aren't you my long lost brother?"
and Pecos Bill is like "NO.
I AM A COYOTE.
AWOOOO."
And his brother is like "Bullshit.
If you are a coyote, then where's your tail?"
And Pecos Bill is like "Hmm, tough question.
Well, I definitely have fleas, AND I howl at the moon."
And his brother is like "Son
EVERYONE in Texas has fleas and howls at the
    moon.
Also, you clearly speak English and walk on two legs
both of which are suspiciously un-coyote-like
even in Texas.
Now cut the bullshit
put on this hat
and come be a cowboy like me."
And Pecos Bill is like "Okay, you talked me into it."
So he becomes the best cowboy ever.
He invents branding cattle
and also sitting on cattle until they behave
and also the lasso
and his brother is like "Not bad
for some crazy asshole who thought he was a coyote for
    fifteen years.
Keep practicing, kid.
Some day you'll be a great cowboy."
And he turns out to be TOTALLY RIGHT.

Which just goes to reinforce the point I've been
    making
which is that Pecos Bill
is clearly not the hero of this story
(just like Paul Bunyan was not the hero of his story
and John Henry was not the hero of HIS story)
because without his brother
Pecos Bill would have farted around that river
with a pack of rabid coyotes
until some poacher found this naked dirt-streaked
    thing
fucking a she-coyote in the underbrush
and put an end to his special crazytime.

See, this is what the United States of America is all
    about.
You can wrestle a thousand bears
and chew on a billion knives
but in the end, you are only as good
as the dude who stops you from dying of a gunshot
while fucking a coyote.

◆ ◆ ◆

DAVY CROCKETT
TALKS A BIG GAME

DAVY
DAAAAVY CROCKETT
HE'S GOT A DONG THAT'S EIGHT MILES
    LONG
HE KILLED LIKE A MIIIILLION BEARS

AND HE'S SUCH A BIG PIMP THAT HE GOT
    HIS OWN SONG.
Yes, ladies and gentlemen
you are about to hear about the rootinest, tootinest
alligator-shootinest son of a gun
ever to be a *United States Congressman*?
Yep, I'm talking about Davy Crockett, apparently.
It's okay, I didn't know he was a congressman either
but I guess it's not particularly surprising
given our history, re: guns.

We'll get to the politics part later, though.
Right now, let's talk about this guy's childhood.
So first of all, it is a well-established, canonical fact
that Davy Crockett killed his first bear
when he was THREE YEARS OLD.
Then they tried to put him in school
but he ran away
because he was afraid that he might mistake his fellow
    students for bears
and then MURDER THEM.
Just kidding
Davy Crockett was never afraid of anything
he just had trouble fitting his massive balls through the
    schoolhouse door.

Anyway, his dad gets pretty mad at him after that
mainly because he's jealous of his son's megaballs
so Davy Crockett runs away and kills more bears
maybe he gets raised by wolves
or maybe he raises some wolves himself
and that is why wolves are so hard-core now
but either way he eventually comes back home
just in time to handle his dad's shit for him
because his dad sucks at business.
Then he runs for Congress and WINS

(on his second try).
He remains a congressman for several terms, on
    and off
during which time he does nothing but make threats
    and animal noises.
Seriously, here's a quote:
"Who-Who-Whoop—Bow-Wow-Wow-Yough."
This is the kind of stunning oratory Davy Crockett's
    constituents come to expect.
And eventually people get tired of this, and Davy fails
    to get reelected
so he tells everyone to go to hell
(including his wife and kids)
and then HE goes to the next best place:
Texas.

Now at this time, Texas was kind of a fiasco.
It was this great big swath of furious gunfire
trying real hard to be its own country
and Mexico was making this real hard
by supplying a large amount of the gunfire.
Remember I told you about the gunfire before?
Yeah, this is one of the places where the gunfire is
    happening.
So Davy Crockett shows up with thirty well-armed
    bad boys ready to take on the world
or at least Mexico, which is really what they need in
    Texas at that moment
and he makes some speeches to his adoring public
like about how he can "walk like an ox
run like a fox
swim like an eel
yell like an Indian
fight like a devil
spout like a geyser
make love like a mad bull

and swallow a Mexican whole without choking
if you butter his head and pin his ears back."
Wait, never mind. That's just another one of his
    speeches from Congress.

Speeches or no speeches, it's not too long before Davy
    Crockett ends up at the ALAMO
and we all know what happens at the Alamo, don't we?
Wait, you don't?
Are you telling me
YOU DON'T REMEMBER THE ALAMO?
Well basically, there's this bad, bad dude
called General Santa Ana
and he is romping and stomping his way
from Mexico into Texas
to make Texas into Mexico
and right smack-dab in the path of Santa Ana's army
is this old church called the Alamo
which has been turned into a fortress
and filled with Texan dudes.
The Texan dudes aren't doing too well, though
because there aren't that many of them
so Davy Crockett sees this as a perfect opportunity
to back up some of that ridiculous game he's been
    talking
and he brings his thirty guys to the Alamo
and they put up a good fight
but they still all get killed
including Davy Crockett, who dies surrounded by
    SIXTEEN DEAD MEXICANS
only one of which he appears to have stabbed
so I imagine he just stared all those other dudes down.
Then Santa Ana's troops keep on marching
but they are so demoralized by having removed such a
    legit badass from the world
that they are pretty easy to kill after that.

Later, Disney makes a movie out of Davy Crockett's
    life!

So the moral of the story
is by all means, talk the talk
but think twice before you walk the walk
because you might get shot.

◆ ◆ ◆

THIS IS WHAT TOM
CRUISE BELIEVES IN

So there's this guy Xenu, right?
He is this seriously bad dude
who also happens to be the emperor
of a MASSIVE GALACTIC EMPIRE.
The empire is made up of like twenty-six stars
and seventy-six planets
one of which is Earth
except we can't call it Earth
because that doesn't sound dumb enough.
No
let's call it Teegeeack.

So this galactic civilization
is pretty much like Earth from the '50s and '60s
in fact, it is basically exactly the same.
Everyone wears the same clothes
and they have cars and buses and stuff.
Not a very advanced galactic civilization, actually.
BUT WAIT:

Xenu is about to get deposed
for being a seriously bad dude all the time
but then he realizes
that if he just kills all the dudes who want to depose
    him, he can't get deposed!
Here is the problem with that plan, though:
EVERYONE WANTS TO DEPOSE XENU.
So he's like "Well, I guess I'd better kill everyone.
But I'm going to need some help.
HEY, PSYCHIATRISTS?
I need you to trick all these people
or rather, all these THETANS
(because that is what these guys are called)
into showing up to my place for a tax audit or
    something."
And the psychiatrists are like
"We have no problem with this, because we are evil."
So all the Thetans show up to get their taxes
    audited . . .

Actually, hold on.
Why is it
that everyone in the galaxy shows up
for an INCOME TAX AUDIT?
Especially if we are postulating
that these guys have the technology of the 1950s
which did not include faster-than-light travel
as far as I can tell
so people are traveling HUNDREDS OF YEARS
in their shitty, explosion-prone spacecraft
for an INCOME TAX AUDIT.
Now if it had been a free-puppies-and-cotton-candy
    audit, maybe I could see this working
but if you want to depose a guy
and then he is suddenly like "HEY
HOW 'BOUT THOSE INCOME TAXES."

Your response should not be "RIGHT AWAY, SIR,
CAN I CRADLE YOUR BALLS AS WELL?"

Where were we?
Oh yeah.
As might be expected, this whole thing turns out really
    badly for the Thetans.
I mean, as soon as they show up
Xenu freezes them in alcohol and takes their souls
and then he puts them in some spaceships
and takes them to Earth
wait, wait, no . . . sorry . . .
TEEGEEACK
and he stacks them around active volcanoes.
But active volcanoes
are not naturally dangerous enough for Xenu.
so he drops HYDROGEN BOMBS in all of the
    volcanoes
vaporizing all these Thetans
but . . . keeping their souls intact?
Then Xenu forces all these Thetan souls
into a massive 3-D movie theater
where they watch a thirty-six-hour movie
encompassing all future religious symbolism.
And where is this movie theater located exactly?
Hawaii.
OBVIOUSLY.
Only a true evil mastermind would stage a massive
    campaign of subliminal mind torture
in the future birthplace
of PRESIDENT BARACK OBAMA.

All right, you with me so far?
Good.
So when the Thetans get let out of the movie theater
they are so crazy disoriented

that they just start grab-assing at any body they can
    find
turning perfectly functional human beings
into worthless sadness engines
bent on self-destruction
and THAT'S why we all suck so bad, see?
It is because a supervillain put bombs in
volcanoes and then evil spirits laid eggs in our minds.

This is an actual religion, guys
made up by an actual dude.
His name is L. Ron Hubbard
and he is actually a science-fiction writer
and he calls this religion SCIENTOLOGY
and this religion makes something like five hundred
    million dollars a year.

But the worst part
is that if you try and learn all this stuff
without first preparing yourself to learn it
by paying a lot of money again and again
the shock will be so great that you will get pneumonia.

So the moral is
don't read this myth
    unless you want to get pneumonia.

CONCLUSION

The Prevailing Creation Myth

Here's one more to go out on:

So back in the back in the back in the back in the back
    in the day
there was this tiiiiny ball of all the matter in the
    universe, and that's ALL there was.
But don't be fooled by its size, my friends.
This matter
was DENSE.
Denser than the beats issuing from the most legitimate
    of subwoofers.
Denser than the skull of world headbutt champion
    Maxx "The Russian Concussion" Headbutts
Denser than the cream of a coconut banana cream pie
on the face of a clown who is going for the world record
    for most pies to the face.
This matter was DENSE.
Where did it come from?

Who knows!
That's not important right now.
What's important is that at some point
all this matter gets REALLY sick
of hanging out with the same matter all the time
so it does what matter does best
or at least, most awesomely:
IT EXPLOOOODES.

Now, friends
I have seen some explosions in my life.
All of them were sweet.
Some of them I might even call DOUBLE SWEET
but nothing can top an explosion SO INTENSE
that it is still going on
ALMOST FOURTEEN BILLION YEARS LATER.
That is why, to this day, if you look through a telescope
you are going to see the rest of the universe
hauling ass away from you.
Anyway, lemme backtrack a little.

So after exploding as hard as it can for a real long time
all the matter turns into particles
called electrons, protons, and neutrons
and all these particles get a little lonely
and start looking for other particles to hook up with.
And when they get together
they pull some Voltron shit and turn into ELEMENTS
like hydrogen and helium and stuff.
Then all the hydrogen gets together and is like "Hey
I know we were all just exploding as hard as possible a
    minute ago
but you know what would be cool?
If we exploded EVEN HARDER."
So they turn into STARS

and then their explosions produce a bunch of other
    elements, which form big clouds around them
and then those clouds get hit by MORE explosions
from when other stars became TOO EXTREME
and they start spinning so fast
that the elements get all frisky with each other
and turn into less explode-y balls of stuff
like planets, mainly
and one of those planets is EARTH.

But Earth was not always sweet beach parties and
    rock-and-roll music, my friends.
No, Earth used to be 100 percent MAGMA
with volcanoes going off
ALL THE TIME
AND THEN AN ASTEROID SLAMS INTO IT
AND RIPS A BIG CHUNK OF IT OFF INTO
    SPACE
AND THAT
is where the moon comes from.
But then Earth gets older and chills out a little
and forms an atmosphere out of steam and volcano spit
and it gets a bunch of water by being constantly
    bombarded by GIANT BALLS OF ICE
and for some reason, all of this adds up
to make it a hospitable place for things to live.

So little things start living there
they come from space, or from Earth
depending on who you ask.
They mainly start out in the big water parts
(which cover most of everything
just like in the Native American creation myths
and the Egyptian creation myth
and that part in the Bible where God gets real pissed)

And these little things learn this really neat trick
which is how to make more of themselves
using CHEMICAL REACTIONS
except . . .
chemical reactions aren't always accurate
so sometimes they make really gross, messed-up
    versions of themselves
and sometimes
they make PROTOZOIC SUPERHEROES.
So the messed-up versions die
and the superheroes get to make more superheroes
and eventually someone figures out how to have legs
and then they get curious about this whole land thing
and they crawl onto it
and then there are DINOSAURS, but they die
and then later, people!

Now, I know what you're probably thinking:
You're probably thinking
"Wait a second, this isn't a myth.
This is science!"
Well, yes and no.
See, this
is a story
and like most stories, the most important thing
isn't whether it's true or not
the most important thing
is whether it gives us a satisfying explanation
of what we see in the world
and maybe some rudimentary means
of predicting what will happen next.
That's all any of these myths have been trying to do:
to take a huge, terrifying phenomenon
something you can only stare at and go "whoa"
and turn it into something more our size

something we can fit inside our puny brains.
Something really cool, even:
a story.

Me, I don't see much of a difference between Science
    and Religion.
First off, in order to successfully *apply* science
there are always going to be certain things that you're
    taking on faith
like that the universe behaves rationally
or that the accumulation of knowledge is a good thing.
Without those assumptions
you end up like that Descartes dude
unable to prove anything except that you exist
which is just boring.
And I mean, the first natural philosophers
(the Greek dudes who are widely credited with getting
    the whole science thing rolling)
were offering theories that sounded a lot like myths.
"The world is a bunch of islands floating on water!"
"We live on the back of a space turtle, in space!"
And those explanations were discarded
as more satisfying ones came along
just like how no one really worships Zeus anymore
because they've found gods more compelling
than a big adulterer who shoots lightning.
Some people say
    that it's that willingness to reject discredited views
that willingness to *change*
that makes science different from religion.
I'd say that that willingness to change
is just a tenet of the religion of science.
Hell, voodoo's gone through an awful lot of changes too
and a Taoist monk systematically unlearns his world
    knowledge

as fast as any scientist can learn it.

Now, I'm not trying to undermine the importance of
    science
personally, I'm all about it.
And I'm not saying I think Creationism and Evolution
should be taught side by side in schools.
Largely because Creation Science is taught
as an aggressive argument against evolution
as opposed to something that stands on its own.
Plus it misuses a lot of the methodology of science
in a very misleading way
without accepting most of the founding principles
which would be a lot like coming up
with a basic theory of Christianity
based on the assumption that God doesn't exist
and that anyone who thinks he does is an asshole.

No, see what I'm trying to say
    is that I watch people organizing themselves
into these neat little conflicts:
Atheists versus Christians
Jews versus Muslims
Fundamentalists versus basically everybody
and I feel like a kid in a broken home
who can't get Mom and Dad to stop fighting.
The assumption
that every one of these groups is making—
and I think it's important to acknowledge
that *every group*, from scientist to Sikh, assumes this—
is that they are right.
That they are somehow *behaving rationally.*
But the fact that we can get so angry about this stuff
means that it's *not* rational
and I think we could get a hell of a lot further
by synthesizing these beliefs

than by finding more and more nuanced ways
to call each other dicks.

So I guess the moral of the story
is that all you religious people need to stop hating on
    the scientists, and vice versa
because at the end of the day, we are all united
by our desire for sweet explosions.

THE END.

ABOUT THE AUTHOR

Cory O'Brien (aka Ovid Naso)
is a dude who likes myths a whole lot.
When he's not writing them in books
he is usually yelling them at people in bars
or posting them on his website bettermyths.com.
He grew up on top of a hill in Los Angeles, California
where there are basically no myths at all
but where one time a guy got shot in the leg
outside his friend's house
and broke in to use the telephone.
Now he lives in Chicago, Illinois
where it is much colder
but on the other hand
no injured people have broken into his house.
Yet.
He is currently doing an MFA in writing
at the School of the Art Institute of Chicago
not that it shows.
Also, birds really freak him out.
They're like tiny, winged sociopaths.
Seriously, have you ever looked at those things?